# Teaching of Mathematics

Dr. Sanjeev Sonawane
Dr. Kothawade Pravin Laxman

A.P.H. PUBLISHING CORPORATION
4435–36/7, ANSARI ROAD, DARYA GANJ,
NEW DELHI-110002

*Published by*
**S.B. Nangia**
**A.P.H. Publishing Corporation**
4435–36/7, Ansari Road, Darya Ganj,
New Delhi-110002
Phone: 011–23274050
E-mail: aphbooks@gmail.com

2023



*Typeset by*
**Ideal Publishing Solutions**
C-90, J.D. Cambridge School,
West Vinod Nagar, Delhi-110092

*Printed at*
**BALAJI OFFSET**
Navin Shahdara, Delhi-110032

# ACKNOWLEDGMENT

It is by the grace and blessings of the Almighty God Ganesha and my Kuldevata Goddess Ashapuri and Gurudevata Kalavati Mata that the writing of this book has reached to its stage of completion. I bow my head to them for their mercy.

From school life, I have interest in learning of Mathematics. I decided to become a teacher in Mathematics after B.Sc. I got chance instantly after B.Ed for teaching to D.Ed. course. From 1991 to 2010 I taught Mathematics to D.Ed., B.Ed. and 5th to 10th class. In this experience period I have handled so many books regarding Teaching of Mathematics in Marathi and English language. One thing I noted that so much new trends are coming in field of education day to day and today's knowledge is becoming stale for tomorrow. Models of Teaching, concept of content cum methodology, special education of Mathematics to special students, computer aided learning, smart board teaching and other concepts like math cad, Geogebra have occupied space to the Mathematics world. So I was thinking about to collect this entire concept with basic concept of mathematics in one book. I shared my concept to my guide and inspiration. Dr. Sanjeev Sonawane regarding this who had a lot of experience in field of writing books on Education and Physical Education; he not only encouraged but also guided to me about which concept should be added to forthcoming book. As he shown the path for writing book on teaching of Mathematics. I started work with his help. After hard work from 2015 now the book on Teaching of Mathematics had now come on the way of completion due to of APH Publication.

The present book is an attempt to organize the subject matter of B.Ed, & four year integrated B.Sc.B.Ed. Course of different Universities. It will be helpful not only for trainee teacher but also to the in-service teachers, teacher educators, researchers and other students of teacher – training institutions.

I extremely be hold to my respected Principal Nankar M. L. who is a pillar of strength in my work through all. My son Shubham Kothawade and my uncle Ramkrishna Kothawade deserve special thanks for helping D.T.P. typing and setting of this book. I express my sincere gratitude to a number of worthy colleagues of my B.Ed. College and well wishers for their valuable suggestions, cooperation and moral support. Thanks to the APH publisher for bringing out this book timely and in good shape.

I expect that the student teacher and teacher educators will welcome and appreciate this book as it covers important topics of Teaching of Mathematics which will certainly beneficial to them. Comments and suggestions of the recipients for further improvement of the book will be accepted.

***Dr. Kothawade Pravin Laxman***

# CONTENTS

# Chapter-1

# NATURE OF MATHEMATICS

## 1.1 NATURE, MEANING, SCOPE & IMPORTANCE OF MATHEMATICS AT SECONDARY LEVEL

### 1.1.1 Introduction

Creation of nature and mathematics are closely related. The sun, earth other planets and stars are specific geometrical figures. Thus, the origin of mathematics is hidden in the evolution of nature. On the other hand the natural society curiosity of human being might be considered as the source of origin of mathematics. Human is the most intelligent creature of nature. In all the spheres of life activities, he makes use of his mind. So obiviously at the first stage of his mental development some questions such as what, how and how many might have arisen by seeing the environment and sky, hearing the sound, touching the subject etc. The search for the solutions of questions what and why? originated the spiritual branches of knowledge. The questions how many and how much were concerned with measurement which might have formed the bases for the development of mathematics. To get the solution of these questions the primitive human would have to make an approach of logical reasoning and rational thinking. This logical approach and rational thinking are the bases of mathematics. It clearly indicates that mathematical phenomena prevailed in human being from very beginning. Therefore mathematics is an important aspect of human life and it is all pervasive in every branch of knowledge.

The number is the basic element of mathematics. As stated above, the logical enquiry prevails in human mind from very beginnings. So, the need of knowing or counting the other member of his race might have been left by the first human just after the evolution of second human. So, the mathematics may be considered as the first branch of knowledge or discipline and in this sense it should not be an exaggeration to say that mathematics is the mother of all the disciplines. But the initial source of human life. So, its importance is self-evident.

Thus, it seems that mathematics is evolved from its related concepts and assumptions. It is all pervasive. It is an abstract science but, also deals with concrete objects. Therefore, it is science as well as art. Its limits are endless. It provides basis to all the branches of knowledge whether art or science, has its involvement. For perfection, every discipline has to depend on mathem the limits of mathematics and to put it under a perfect definition but, its nature, fundamental elements, method of study, scope and some definitions are the basis to develop insight in the subject. So, it is desirable to have a look on these bases to understand the mathematics and its various aspects.

### 1.1.2 Meaning of Mathematics

The term 'Mathematics' has been interpreted and explained in various ways. This is due to our empirical knowledge and various types of experiences. But ultimately all types of explanations conclusively end at some kinds of relations with number and space. Mathematics is a very important subject. Therefore, before imparting and transmitting its knowledge, it is necessary to understand that, 'What is mathematics?' Why its knowledge is given? And 'What is its nature?' No one definition of mathematics is universally accepted. Generally there are many definitions of mathematics for example; some define mathematics as a science of calculation, some as a science of measurement, magnitude and direction. Infact, the meaning of word mathematics is 'The science in which calculations are prime.' In this way on the basis of these assumptions of mathematics, we can say that mathematics is the science of numbers, word, sign, etc. with which we can know about magnitude, direction & space. To understand its meaning more clearly, let us have a view on some definitions given by great scholars and mathematicians.

**Definitions of mathematics**

According to New English Dictionary -"Mathematics in a strict sense, is the abstract science which investigates deductively the conclusions implicit in the elementary conceptions of spatial and numerical relations."

In Hindi, Mathematics is known as 'GANITA' meaning there by - 'The science of calculations.' The Term Mathematics can be defined in numerous ways to quote oxford dictionary-"Mathematics is the science of measurement, quantity and magnitude."

**Some other definition**

**In the words of Locke,** "Mathematics is a way to settle in the mind of children a habit of reasoning."

**According to Roger Bacon,** "Mathematics is the
gate and key of sciences. ........
Neglect of mathematics
work injury to all knowledge, since who is ignorant of it cannot know the other sciences or the things of world. And what is worse, men who are thus ignorant are unable to perceive their own ignorance and so do not seek a remedy."

**According to Bertrand Russell -** "Mathematics may be defined as the subject in which we never know what we are talking about, nor whether what we are saying true."

**Benjamin Peirce-** "Mathematics is the science that draws necessary conclusions."

**Galileo -** "Mathematics is the language in which God has written the universe."

According to Mathematician, "Mathematics may be defined as the science of number and space."

These definitions of mathematics can be put into some specific categories to explain the concept of number and space.

(*a*) Mathematics as the science of magnitude and numbers.

(*b*) Mathematics as the science of quantity and space

(*c*) Mathematics as an important means of generalization.

(*d*) Mathematics as an applied science for the expression of other sciences.

(*e*) Mathematics as the method of progress of various subjects.

(*f*) Mathematics as the means to draw conclusions and judgment.

(*g*) Mathematics as the perfection of generalization.

(*h*) Mathematics as the science of logical reasoning.

The definition under last category is most accepted and widely used. The definitions under other categories may easily be accommodated in this category.

Therefore it can be said that the mathematics is a systematized, organized and exact branch of science.

### 1.1.3 Nature of Mathematics

What is Mathematics and how does it grow are the basic questions which all the students of mathematics must understand. In school, those subjects which are included in the curriculum must have certain aims and objectives on the basis of which its nature is decided. Mathematics holds a strong and unbreakable position as compared to other subjects. With this reason, mathematics is more stable and important than other school subjects.

The nature of any subjects depends on its structure which determines the predictive value of the subject. The degree of true prediction signifies the strongness of the structure of the subjects. Mathematical predictions are almost accurate and cent-percent true. This is due to strong structure of mathematics based on sound foundation. Nature of mathematics can be explained by discussing it under following heads-

1. Mathematics as a science of discovery
2. Mathematics as an Intellectual game
3. Mathematics as art of drawing conclusions

4 Mathematics as a tool subject

5 Mathematics as a system of logical Process

6 Mathematics as a Intuitive Method

## 1 Mathematics as a science of discovery

Bacon said, 'Mathematics is a gate and key all sciences.' This means that mathematics as a tool especially suited for dealing with scientific concepts and in scientific concept experiency of the Joy & discovery is very important. Its starts from observation later when Power of abstraction develops it makes student to able to appreciate the attitude & mathematical conclusion. This gives the joy of discovering mathematical truth and concept.

Students of secondary must not only have opportunities for making their own discoveries of mathematical ideas but they must also have the Practice necessary to achieve accuracy in their calculations.

## 2 Mathematics as an Intellectual game

Mathematics can be treated as an Intellectual game with its own rules and without any relation to external criteria. From this view point mathematics is mainly a matter of Puzzles, Paradoxes and problem solving - a sort of healthy material exercise

## 3 The art of Drawing couclusious

One of Important functions of the school is to familiarize children with mode of thought which helps them in drawing right conscious and Interferences. For this purpose in mathematics, student of secondary learns that where or not he has drawn the correct conclusions.

It permits the learner to begin with simple and very easy conclusions to pass in well graded sequence to very different ones as the earlier ones are mastered due to this characteristics, mathematics to a large extent than in any other available subject of the art of drawing conclusions.

## 4 As a tool subject

From the beginning, down to the nineteenth century mathematics has been assigned the status of a servant. Then in the nineteenth century mathematics attained independence. It achieved completeness and internal consistency that it has not known before. Mathematics continued to be useful to other discipline, but now it is dependent upon none of them. With its new found freedom, mathematics established its own goals to pursue. Its mentors of the past engineering, physical science and commerce-now become no more than its peers.

## 5 Mathematics - A system of logical process

Mathematics actually has two faces one face is systematic deductive science and second is hypothetic deductive system. This means that mathematics is a system of logic processes whereby conclusions are deducted from certain fundamental assumption and definitions that have been hypothesised.

e.g. "When two line Intersects, vertically opposite angles are equals" (the premise)

$\angle$A or $\angle$D are vertically opposite angels.

Hence $\angle$A and $\angle$D are equal (the inference)

This conclusion is deducted from the premise 'vertically opposite angels are equal'. Thus the process of deduction involves two steps; first, replacing the real premises by hypothetical ones; second, making a mathematical inference from the hypothetical working premises. Therefore to think mathematically is to free oneself by abstraction from any pecusd liarity of subject matter and to make interference amd deductions justified by fundamental premises. It involves logical reasoning. By reasoning we prove that if something is true then something else must be true. Hence through mathematics of secondary and higher secondary logical responding skill develops in students.

## 6 Mathematics An Intuitive method

The first step in the learning of any mathematical subject is the development of intuition. This must come before rules are stated or formal operations are introduced. The teacher has to faster intuition in our young children by following rights strategies of teaching.

Intuition when applied to mathematics involves the concretization of an idea and yet stated in the form of done sort of operation or example. Intuition is to anticipate what will happen next and what to do about it. It is up to the teacher to allow the child to use his natural and intuitive ways of thinking by encouraging him to do so and honoring him when he does.

## 7 Mathematics Deals with generalization and classification

Mathematics provides simple exercises in combining various results under one head in marking schematics arrangement and classification when the pupils evolves his own definitions, concepts and thermos, he is making generalizations. The generalizations and classifications of mathematics are very simple and obvious in comparison with those of other domain of thought and activity. However the mathematics teacher should take care to see that the final generalizations into a rule should always be deferred until it is almost spontaneously suggested by the pupils themselves.

## 8 Mathematical language and symbolism

The language for communication of mathematical ideas is largely in terms of symbols and words which everybody cannot understands. There is no popular terminology for talking about mathematics.

The symbol of mathematics constitutes a language which is gradually developed by and for the pupil. Long period of training with patience and endurance is needed to more the student feels at home with this language. The training that mathematics provides in the use of symbols is an excellent preparation for other science.

The use of symbols makes the mathematics language more elegant and precise than any other language for example the commutative law of addition and multiplication in real number system can be stated in the verbal from as; ' the addition and multiplication of two real numbers is independent of the order in which they are combined'. This can be stated in a concise from as $a+b = b+a$ and

$a \times b = b \times a$, a & b $\in$ R. Almost all mathematics statements; relations and operations are expressed using mathematics symbols like +, -, x, -, =, <, >, @, p, ~,e,V, Z.....And so on.

### 9 Mathematics is an Abstract science

Mathematical concepts are abstract in the sense that they cannot be seen or felt in the physical world for example Euclid's lines are supposed to have no width and his points have no size. No such objects can be found in the physical world. Infinity is something that we can never experience and yet it is a central concept of mathematics. Similarly negative numbers do not correspond to any physical objectives because we can't have quantities less than nothing.

## 1.1.4 Scope of mathematics at Secondary Level

Mathematics is all Pervasive. So the demarcation of its scope is difficult task, if not impossible. It is science of all sciences and provides basis to all the disciplines. According to this definition it is science of all sciences and provides basis to all the disciplines two main aspects or categories of mathematics are 'Basic Mathematics' & Applied Mathematics.

### A Basics Mathematics or Pure Mathematics

The theoretical aspect of mathematics is termed as basic mathematics or pure mathematics. It involves systematic & deductive reasoning. It treats only theories and Principles without regard to their application to concrete things. It consist of all those assertions as that if such and such another proposition is true of that thing. It is developed on an abstract self contained basic without any regard to possible practical application that may follow. The following are sub branches of pure mathematics.

(*a*) **Algebra** - It includes arithmetic, elementary & multivariable algebra, linear multivariable Algebra, Algebraic structure etc.

(*b*) **Geometry** - It includes Euclidean & non Euclidean geometry, projection analytic geometry trigonometry, combinatorial geometry, differential and algebrical geometry etc.

(*c*) **Modern Mathematics -** It consist of following topics

(*i*) Set theory- origin & definition, fundamental set topic, Contorian set theory, Postulates of axiomatic set theory, the present status of axiomatic set theory etc.

(*ii*) Topology- General topology, topological groups, differential topology, Algebraic topology

(*iii*)Algebraic system- Groups, rings, fields, vector spaces etc.

(*d*) Analysis - It includes real & complex analysis, functional analysis, Different equations, Theory of Probability, vector & tensor

**B Applied Mathematics**

Applied mathematics is the application of pure mathematics in developing the various means to serve the human & humanity. Principles of applied mathematics have been used to investigate phenomenon such as heat, light, electricity, sound, mechanics, astronomy etc. Thus it helps in solving the intricate problems of physical or real world it also has various sub- branches.

The following are sub-branches of applied mathematics -

(*a*) Calculatory Science- It includes numerical notations, calculatory aspects of algebra, calculatory use of table & graphs, geometrical aids,mathematical models, analogic computation, digital computation etc.

(*b*) Statistics - Basic principles, Estimation, Hypothesis testing structure etc.

(*c*) Numerical Analysis -

(*d*) Mathematical theory of Optimization-

(*e*) Automation theory-

(*f*) Mathematical aspects of physical theories it includes

(*i*) Mechanics of Solid, Fluids, Particles & system

(*ii*) Quantum mechanics

(*iii*)Theory of Relativity

(*iv*) Dimensional Analysis

## 1.1.5 Place of Mathematics at Secondary Level

In the curriculum, mathematics occupies an important place. In the most of states of our country mathematics is taught as compulsory subject up to higher secondary or secondary stage. Secondary education is minimum requirement for life. After completing this education some students enter into life while others go in for higher education It is on account of this fact it has suggested that the curriculum at the secondary stage should be terminus as well as preparatory & should compramise of mathematics.

It certain states of India mathematics is compulsory subject up to Junior and High School or middle School standard only, education in these stages could not be complete without some knowledge of mathematics.

**Mathematics as an optional subject in higher secondary.**

In our state, upto $10^{th}$ standards, means up to secondary stage mathematics is a compulsory subject & in Higher secondary education, it is not compulsory. Only those students study mathematics who have a desire to persue some specialized Vocation or Profession. This is correct in the sense that everybody is not expected to apply Higher mathematical in everybody life.

**Compulsion of mathematics at Secondary & Higher Secondary levels.**

Everybody stands in need of some mathematical knowledge. But in the case of an ordinary citizen it is felt that the knowledge acquired during the preliminary & middle stage will suffice. Consequently there is some controversy over the place of mathematical in the school curriculum.

One who believes that mathematics should be made optional at the high school stage; the other who argues that it should be compulsory one; idea & arguments put forward by both sides seem to be equally sound. Promoter of optional side suggest that everybody after his High School education is not going to be a scientist of an engineer or anybody to whom the facts of mathematics are necessary for future works more ever they argue that it should be optional at the High School Stage because in most of the democratic countries like England and America it is optional. Thirdly, they argue that as in other countries a man who has learnt mathematics up to middle class is capable of earning his living. It is also possible in our country the argument put forward by these gentleman appear to be sound. But they do not see to the other side of the picture. Can they or anybody else prophesy or judge whether who is going to be engineer or a mechanic? If we cannot judge; it is our duty to provide to the student a broad view of what many ways in the future & give him a better course to enable him to judge for himself. As to his best a better course to enable him to judge for himself as to his best line of endeavor & not to make him regret his early choice.

Argument regarding optional as it is so in foreign countries is also baseless, the term 'mathematics' and 'Secondary and Higher Secondary' do not have the same meaning there as we, in India attach to it Secondary & Higher

Secondary level student in those country corresponds to the Intermediate students of our country & the mathematics that they want to make optional in their school is much higher both in quality & quantity.

It will be possible to make Mathematics as an optional at Secondary & Higher Secondary level. If we have same standard of the students as in those countries.

### 1.1.6 Importance of Mathematics at Secondary Level

Mathematics is mother of all science. If our students are to function effectively in this era & repaid technological advancement and globalization, they must be mathematically literate. Those who understand and can do mathematics have significantly enhanced opportunities and option the open doors to productivity.

In the words of Young "It (mathematics) is the only subject that encourages and develops logical thinking. It enables the student to discriminate between essential and non essential. It helps them to sift facts to draw conclusions tersely and without ambiguity and that is the subject by which they may learn what is meant by right resoning".

Therefore knowledge of mathematics is very essential for training rational trust worthy and useful citizens in a democratic society.

When we think about importance of mathematics as secondary and higher secondary level students it is as following -

1. A good mathematical background with the knowledge of concept and theories is essential for meeting the challenges of the modern technological society.
2. The study of mathematics develops the ability to transfer the mathematical types of thinking and resolving to daily life.
3. Mathematics helps to appreciate the application of mathematics for the sociality and technological advancement.
4. Mathematics learning at secondary and higher secondary level helps for better understanding of the world around us.
5. The slowly of mathematics at secondary and higher secondary develops ability to make independent decisions in social issues.
6. Learning of mathematics develops ability to transfer the knowledge and skill learned through mathematics lessons to context in the work place and in everyday life.
7. Mathematics of Secondary and Higher Secondary level helps the students to future those who have to do carrier in the field of IIT, Engineering Computer
& IT
8. Mathematics at Secondary and Higher Secondary level helps to think alternative methods of solving problems..

Mathematics study enhances the ability to apply mathematical ideas and relationship areas outside classroom such as art, science & other curricular areas and in everyday's life, especially physical phenomena

## 1.2 OBJECTIVES OF TEACHING MATHEMATICS FOR THE TEACHER AT SECONDARY LEVEL

For the teacher it is practically impossible to realize all the aims of mathematics education within the frame work of curriculum, for this they involve a total Programme of education encompassing even out of classroom experience. The part of the aim that can be achieved without an instruction (or in a classroom) is an objective while aims give direction to education; objectives are directed towards the aim.

### WHAT IS AN OBJECTIVE-?

### 1.2.1 Meaning

An Instructional objective is a statement of expected result; It is a description of the learning outcome that the teacher hopes with result from the instruction whether in a lesson unit or course. It is a statement of what students should be able to do at the end of learning period that they could not do before hand that thus term objective may be defined as :-

An objective is a point or end view of the possible achievement in terms of what a student is a able to do when the whole educational system is directed towards educational aims.

Thus an objective is a part of the aim which a school can hope to achieve. Hence an objectives is a narrower term which compared to an aim. This can be illustrated as shown in **figure 1.1**

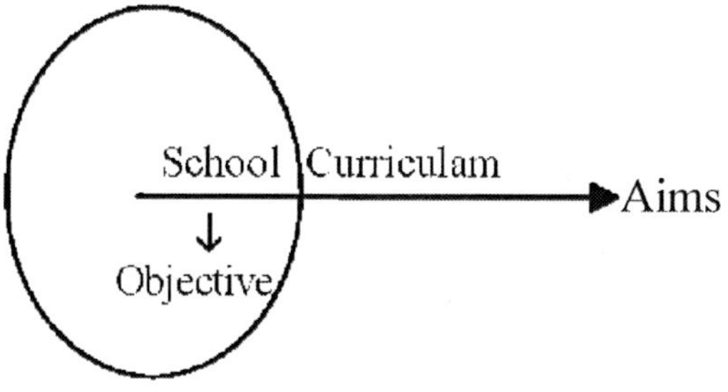


**Figure 1.1**

An instructional objective is a statement that describes what the pupil will do or be able to do towards the realization of an educational aim. In other words an objective is a statement of the terminal behavior expected of the pupil at the conclusion of a period learning

**Example**

1. The student is able to discriminate among mathematical Terms, Symbols, Concepts, Principles, and Generalizations etc.
2. The student is able to explain thermos in mathematics.
3. The student is able to classify postulates, axioms & theorems in mathematics.

### 1.2.2 Need for Stating Objectives

If teaching is planned based on the curriculam alone, then the emphasis is on the teacher's performance.The teacher is more concerned with." What Knowledge can I dictate to the student"? Or "How can I cover the syllabus"? When we use objective that define the outcome of the student learning or expected Performance at the end of course of, then the focus of the teaching learning process gets shifted to the students. A teacher process can then get answer to such questions as

- How can the students grow and change through acquiring & using knowledge & information?
- How is the student who has finished this course different form one who has not taken it?
- What can the student do with their knowledge after they have finished their course?

The instructional objects gives directions to the teacher in designing her instruction, guide the examiner in selecting suitable evaluation technique & helps the student in knowing what is expected of them after completing the Period of learning

**Source of objective**

The following are the source of objectives and the teacher can make use of these sources while writing objectives.

- Aims of Education.
- Instructional aim.
- Aims of mathematics education.
- Opinions of subject experts and association.
- The nature of the learner, and the course of subject.
- The psychology of learning and Teaching
- List of the object developed by SCERT and NCERT

### 1.2.3 Classification of Objectives

Dr. Benjamin Bloom (1956) has classified the changes of behavior in three categories or domain

1. ***Cognitive domain***
2. ***Affective domain***
3. ***Psychomotor domain***

All these three domain are interrelated as shown in figure below

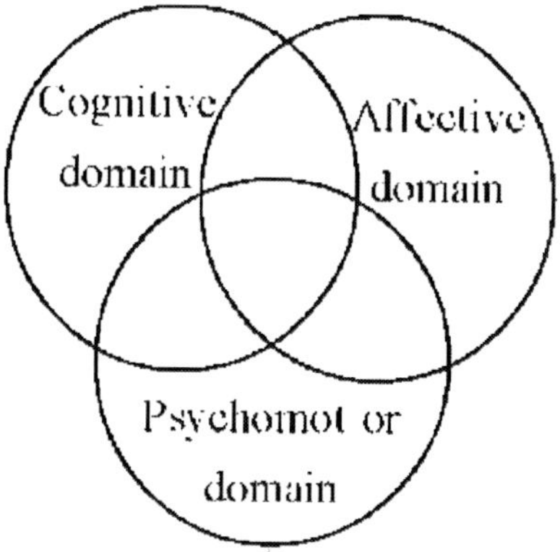


**Figure 1.2**

Dr. Bloom and his associates in the University of Chicago gave the classification of objectives of all the three months.

1. Classification of cognitive domain or objectives by Bloom (1956)
2. Affective domain by Krathwohl (1964) and
3. Psychomotor domain by Simpson (1969).

Dr. Bloom concentrated on the study of cognitive domain. It assumed that in thinking about a problem of hierarchy of cognitive process is involved. While teaching, a teacher follows this hierarchal order. This classification of objectives is known as "Taxonomy of educational objectives or Blooms Taxonomy" of objectives.

**Taxonomy of Teaching Objectives**

| Sr. No. | Cognitive Domain Category | Affective Domain Category | Psychomotor Domain Category |
|---|---|---|---|
| | **Dr.B.S.Bloom(1956)** | **Krathwohl (1964)** | **Simpson (1969)** |
| 1 | Knowledge | Receiving | Impulsion |
| 2 | Comprehension | Responding | Manipulation |
| 3 | Application | Valuing | Control |
| 4 | Analysis | Conceptualization | Co-ordination |
| 5 | Synthesis | Organization | Naturalization Habit |
| 6 | Evaluation | Characterization | formation |

1. **Cognitive Objective -** Cognitive objective stress that the student should acquire more and more and more knowledge. It was defined to include all those activities which deal with the recall or recognition of knowledge and the development of intellectual abilities and skills.
2. **Affective Objective -** Affective objective is connected with the aptitude, interest, emotions, values, and mental tendencies of the pupils. This part of the taxonomy also includes appreciations and social adjustment of the child.
3. **Psychomotor Objective -** This is the third part of taxonomy and includes the manipulative and Motor-skill areas. The physical actions and involved in handwriting, playing, using outline, drawing figures and many others are in the psycho-motor domain.

Bloom defined six main categories in the hierarchy, each higher step encompassing those below. These were in an ascending order of difficulty. The hierarchy of cognitive objective is shown below.

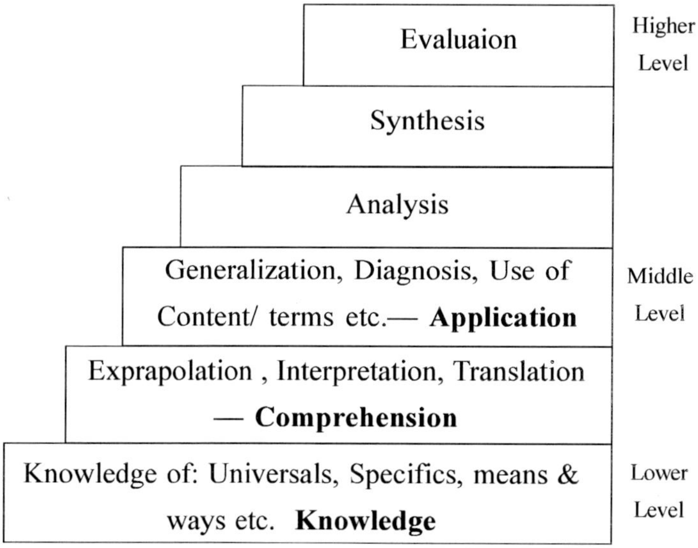


**Hierarchy of Cognitive Objectives**

## Writing Objectives in terms of pupil's Behavior -

After Selection and formulation of objectives the next step is to define or write then to specific terms in relation to what the student can do? We should bring about some specific change in what the children act, feel and think? These are the changes that indicate how far that objective has been achieved. such changes are known as "behaviour or action patterns" or "Pupil's behavioural changes"

It must be noted that that identification and determination of objectives is not an end. It is also essential to define them in terms of pupil's behaviour. Defining objectives means "making the specifications of objectives in simple language," Therefore; the teacher should make it clear in simple language that 'What changes?' and

'What aspects?' are to be brought in order to achieve the objectives. Thus without defining the objectives in behavioural terms, it would not be clear that 'what changes are to be brought' by pre-determined objectives and "in which areas these changes are to brought?" Hence it is necessary to define objectives in terms of behavioural changes. The objectives in terms of pupil's behavioural changes reveal the learning activities.

While writing objectives in behavioural terms following point should be kept in mind —

- Nature of the obj ectives: knowledge, comprehension, application etc.
- Area or domain of the behaviour: cognitive, affective and psychomotor.
- Specific content area in which behavioural changes are planned to be brought about related with the topic.

**Criteria for Judging the validity of a Behaviour -**

We can say that behaviour is a specification of objective expressed in terms of what the student does. The criteria for judging the validity of a behaviour are as follows—

- It should flow from the objective.
- It should be expressed in terms of what the student can do after the objective has been attained by him.
- It should be realistic from the point of view of the student's mental abilities at that stage.
- It should make explicit and idea which is implicit in the objective.

### 1.2.4 Need and Importance of Writing Objectives in Behavioural Terms

The need and importance for writing objectives in behavioural terms is given below—

- The teacher gets help in selecting teaching strategies.
- It helps in making certain and specific teaching activities.

- Teacher gets help in selecting question for evaluation.
- It helps in selecting Audio-Visual Aids for effective teaching.
- With the help of writing objectives in behavioural terms learning experiences can be determined and measured.
- A balance between teaching and learning can be maintained.
- It helps in the measurement of performances and other activities of the student.
- The teaching-learning process can be made objective centered.
- It helps teacher and student both in differentiating amongst various behaviors.
- The specification of objectives present the complete level of curriculum.

### 1.2.5 Objectives of Teaching Mathematics at Secondary Level

(*i*) To develop thinking and reasoning power of the student.

(*ii*) To develop problem solving attitude of the student.

(*iii*) To develop the sense of accuracy and consistency.

(*iv*) To enable the student to understand the concepts and various problems of mathematics.

(*v*) To enable the student to understand the applications of different branches of mathematics

(*vi*) To develop interest in mathematics

(*vii*) To enable the student to correlate the knowledge of mathematics with other school subjects

(*viii*) To develop the power of concentration and decision making.

(*ix*) To enable the student to understand the symbolic language of mathematics.

(*x*) To help the student to understand the different units of measurement and their application

(*xi*) To create awareness regarding day to day development in the field of mathematics.

**Objectives of Mathematics at secondary level according to National Education Policy 1986 -**

It is also emphasized in National Policy on Education (1986) that at the end of high school stage, a student should achieve the following objectives-

**The student should be able to -**

(*i*) Acquire knowledge and understanding of the terms, concepts, laws, formulae, principles, symbols, and mastery of computation etc.

(*ii*) Acquire other fundamental knowledge that is required in day -to -day life and for higher Education.

(*iii*) Develop the skills of measuring, drawing, demonstrating, estimating, and decision making.

(*iv*) Develop the ability to think, analyze, synthesis, reason, criticize, summarize logically.

(*v*) Appreciate the contribution of mathematicians, particularly great Indian mathematicians.

(*vi*) Appreciate the beauty of mathematics.

(*vii*) Apply mathematical knowledge in their daily life.

(*viii*)Develop necessary skill to work with recent technological devices like calculators, computers, internet etc.

(*ix*) Develop interest in learning mathematics.

**Objectives of Mathematics at secondary level according to 2005's Education policy :**

**To enable the student to :-**

(*i*) Acquire knowledge of mathematical terms, symbols, concepts, principles and the skill of presentation of proofs.

(*ii*) Understands the terms, symbols, concepts, principles, processes and proofs.

(*iii*) Develop the ability to apply mathematical knowledge to solve problems in real life situation.

(*iv*) Develop analytical, logical thinking and problem solving abilities of student.

(*v*) Develop expertise in basic algebraic and arithmetical skills.

(*vi*) Develop skills in drawing geometrical figures, diagrams, graphs, charts etc.

(*vii*) Acquire sufficient mathematical tools and techniques necessary for daily and practical problems in life.

(*viii*) Identify inter-relationship between different parts of the problems and draw logical conclusions.

(*ix*) Consolidate the mathematical knowledge and skill acquired at the secondary level.

(*x*) Develop necessary skills to work with modern technological devices such as calculators and computers.

(*xi*) Develop awareness of the need for national unity, national, national integration and protection of the environment and the observation of small family norms.

**Objectives of Teaching Mathematics**

1. **Objective related to knowledge and understanding —**
   - To develop the sense of counting and place value of numbers.
   - To teach the concept of concept of size and shape of an article or object.
   - To give the knowledge of measurement.
   - To teach four fundamental rules of mathematics.
   - To give the knowledge of whole numbers, prime numbers, frictions etc.
   - To teach tablets.
   - To give the idea of various concepts like L.C.M., H.C.F., Percentage, Unitary method, Simple interest, Profit and loss, area etc.
2. **Objectives related to Skills and abilities—**
   - To develop the skills of reading, writing, and counting,
   - To develop skills of apply fundamental rules of mathematics.

- Development of skills to use the tables.
- To develop the skills to draw different geometrical figures and shapes.
- To develop the skills of measurement and construction.
- To develop the skills of Problem-solving.

**3. Objectives related to personal qualification : To develop;**

- Interest in learning mathematics
- Confidence to solve problems.
- Sense of logical reasoning, critical reasoning and thinking.
- Concentration and regularity.
- Sense of truthfulness and exactness.
- Sense to use mathematical knowledge in their day-to-day life.

**At Middle and Secondary (High School) Stage**

- To develop thinking and reasoning power of the child.
- To develop problem-solving attitude of the children.
- To develop the sense of accuracy and consistency.
- To enable the child to understand the concepts and various problem of mathematics.
- To enable the child to understand the application of different branches of mathematics.
- To make the child logical and critical thinker.
- To develop interest in mathematics.
- To enable the child to correlate the knowledge to mathematics with other school subjects.
- To develop the power of concentration and decision making.
- To enable the child to understand the symbolic language of mathematics.
- To help the child to understand the different units of measurement and their application.
- To make the child creative, constructive and research minded.

- To create awareness regarding day-to-day development in the field of mathematics.

### 1.2.6 Instructional Objectives of mathematics at Secondary Level

The Instructional objectives of teachings mathematical at the Secondary level may be classified as under.

(a) Knowledge (b) Understanding objectives.

(c) Application Objective (d) Skill objectives.

(e) Attitude objectives. (f) Application & interest objectives.

To make students unambiguous & attainable these objectives are further expressed in behavioral terms what the student is expected to active is clearly known to the teacher in the form of desirable behavioral changes. Different objectives along with the relevant behavioral changes are given bellow.

**Objective : (1) Knowledge**

Student acquires knowledge of terms, concepts, symbols, definitions, principles, and formulae of mathematics at secondary stage

**Specifications** - To demonstrate the achievement of above objectives,

**The students**

(*i*) Recalls or reproduces. (ii) Recognizes

**Objective : (2) Understanding**

The student develops understanding of terms concepts, symbols, definitions, principles, and formulae of mathematics at secondary stage.

**specifications**

The students

(*i*) Gives illustrations

(*ii*) Detects errors and correct them.

(*iii*) Compares.

(*iv*) Discriminates between closely concepts.

(*v*) Classifies as per criteria.

(*vi*) Identifies relationship among the given data.

(*vii*) Translates verbal statement into symbolical language and vice-versa

(*viii*)Estimates the results.

(*ix*) Verifies.

**Objective : (3) Application**

Student applies above knowledge and understanding of mathematics to unfamiliar situations (or new problems).

**specifications**

The students

(*i*) Analyses and finds out what is required.

(*ii*) Select appropriate method for solving the problem.

(*iii*) Suggest alternative method.

(*iv*) Generalizes (i.e. reasons inductively)

(*v*) Infers (i.e. reasons deductively)

**Objective : (4) Skill**

To acquire skills of computation, drawing geometrical figures and graphs, reading tables and charts, graphs etc.

Students acquires skill in

(*a*) Computation

(*b*) Drawing geometrical figures and graphs.

(*c*) Reading tables and charts, graphs.

**(a) Computations**

**Specifications-**

Student:

(*i*) Carries out oral calculations with ease and speed. (j) Carries out written calculations with ease and speed.

## (b) Drawing geometrical figures and graphs

**Specifications**

Student:

(*i*) Handles geometrical instruments with ease and profiency.

(*ii*) Measures accurately.

(*iii*) Draws free hand figures with ease.

(*iv*) Draws figure accurately.

## (c) Reading tables and charts, graphs.

**Specifications**

Student:

(*i*) Reads Tables with speed and accuracy.

(*ii*) Interprets graph.

**Objective : (5) Appreciation**

The students appreciate the role of mathematics in day to day life.

**Specifications**

Student:

(*i*) Appreciates the role of mathematics in solving problems of other branches of science,

(*ii*) Appreciates the symmetry of the figures and designs.

(*iii*) Appreciates the development of qualities like exactness through the study of mathematics.

(*iv*) Appreciates the rule of Mathematics in everyday life.

(*v*) Appreciates the rule of Mathematics in understanding his environment.

(*vi*) Appreciates Mathematics as the Science of all Science & art of all arts.

(*vii*) Appreciates the Vocational value of the subject Mathematics

**Objective : (6) Interest**

The student develops interest in mathematics

**Specifications**

Student :

(*i*) Reads literature on mathematics

(*ii*) Shows interest in solving mathematical puzzles.

(*iii*) Takes active participation in mathematical Club,

(*iv*) Reads article related to mathematics in Newspaper, Magazines, and Journals.

(*v*) Takes participation in mathematics competition.

(*vi*) Suggests short cuts for solving problems.

(*vii*) Does additional study of mathematics.

(*viii*)Brings additional problem towards teacher not related to the syllabus.

**Objective : (7) Attitude**

The student acquires positive attitude towards mathematics.

**Specifications**

Student:

(*i*) Always talks with mathematics teacher not only on mathematics but on other subjects also.

(*ii*) Always shows interest on test and competition related to mathematics.

(*iii*) Promotes the activities of mathematics clubs in the school.

(*iv*) Like to be in the company of other student of mathematics.

(*v*) Always tries to help the students who are weak in mathematics.

**Objective : (8) Objective realted to Scientifec attitude-**

The student develops scientific attitude towards through the study of mathematics.

**Specifications**

Student:

(*i*) Accepts a proposition only when logically proved.

(*ii*) Examines all the aspects of a problem.

(*iii*) Points out errors boldly if convinced.

(*iv*) Accepts error boldly

(*v*) Respects opinion of others.

(*vi*) Keeps an open mind and does not regard any argument as final.

(*vii*) Develops habit of logical thinking.

**Objective - 8 Objective related to personality traits**

The students develops traits like;

(*i*) Punctuality

(*ii*) Concentration

(*iii*) Regularity

(*iv*) Accuracy

(*v*) Neatness

Here are some examples are given to write objectives in behavioral terms

**Example : (1) Unit- Quadratic Equation Std.- 10 th**

| No. | Objective | Explanations |
|---|---|---|
| 1. | Knowledge | **Student :-**<br>1. States definition of Quadratic Equation.<br>ii) States method of solving Quadratic Equation. |
| 2. | Understanding | **Student :-**<br>(i) Recognizes the Quadratic Equation ii)Writes the Quadratic Equation in a standard form.<br>(iii) Determines whether the values given against each of Quadratic Equation are roots or not. |

| | | |
|---|---|---|
| 3. | Application | **Student:-**<br>(i) Solves Quadratic Equation by Proper Method.<br>(ii) Solves word problem based on Quadratic Equations. |
| 4. | Skill | **Student:-**<br>(i) Solves Quadratic Equation by Proper Method correctly and in time.<br>(ii) Solves word problem based on Quadratic Equations with ease & speed. |

**Example : (1) Unit - Set Std.- 9 th**

| No. | Objective | Explanations |
|---|---|---|
| 1. | Knowledge | **Student :**<br>**(i)** states definition of Set. ii)states method of writing word examples in Set.<br>(iii) states the types of Sets. |
| 2. | Understanding | **Student :-**<br>(i) states various example of as per type of Set.<br>(ii) Differentiate between finite & Infinite set.<br>(iii) Recognize signs of sets. |
| 3. | Application | **Student:-**<br>(i) Explain concept of Set with appropriate examples.<br>(ii) Solves problem based on Set. |
| 4. | Skill | **Student:-**<br>(i) solves problem on sets by proper method correctly and in time.<br>(ii) Draws Venn diagram of as per example of set correctly and in time. |

## 1.3 CURRICULUM & SYLLABUS OF MATHEMATICS AT SECONDARY LEVEL

### 1.3.1 Concept of Curriculum

Curriculum has been defined differently by many authors and over the years the focus is being shifted from 'course and study' to 'Learning activities and experience'. According to Alberty A. and Alberity E. (1959) Curriculum is the sum of student activities which the school sponsors for the purpose of achieving its objectives. Derek Rowntree in 'A Dictionary of education' (1981) has defined Curriculum as "The total structure of ideas and activity developed by on educational institution to meet the needs of students and to achieve educational aims?" Thus it is clear that Curriculum covers not only the courses of study but also covers all the wider areas of individual and group life.

## Mathematics Curriculum

Mathematics curriculum forms on important part of the school curriculum. The Indian Education commission (1966) emphasized the importance of mathematics in the school curriculum in view of the importance of qualification and the advent of automation and cybernetics in the scientific and industrial revolution.

Mathematics curriculum all those systematically planned activities carried out by the student individually in group with or without the supervision of the teacher inside or outside the classroom/ school with the definite purpose of realizing the aim of objectives of teaching mathematics.

## Principles of Curriculum construction in Mathematics

There are certain basic principles of curriculum planning which should form the basis for the construction of good mathematics curriculum.

They are follows :

### 1. Principle of Child Centeredness

The curriculum shall be based on the present needs and capabilities of the children. The curriculum should help in developing initiative, cooperation and social responsibility among the students. This implies that the curriculum should meet the physical, intellectual, emotional and social needs of the students.

### 2 Provision of fullness of experience for students -

Curriculum should help the student in living a wholesome & self full-filling life. It is should be responsive to the fast of changing realities of life.

### 3 Dynamic & not static

The curriculum should reflect growth and movement of the life. It also accommodate the latest development in mathematics, science & information technology.

### 4 Related to everyday to life

Curriculum should provide sufficient opportunities to the student to relate what they learn in classroom with the daily life experience. The problems and theories that from a part of the mathematics curriculum should be real and should help in solving everyday life problems.

- **Real and Rationalist**

Curriculum should be real and should facilitate rational and original thinking.

- **Useful for Higher Education**

Student aims to go higher & higher education ladder. After primary he joins Secondary & Higher Secondary, collage & university or after professional courses. Therefore Curriculum of mathematics at any stage must cater to the needs of the higher classes.

- **Flexible and elastic**

Curriculum should provide a variety of activities keeping in view the requirement of the students of different communities, regions, (rural & urban) & socio economic starta.

- **Integrated**

The Mathematics curriculum should be in conformity with the curriculum of other subjects. There should be continuity & conference within mathematics well.

The learning of mathematics should help in viewing knowledge as a whole and not as a segment of information.

## Organization of the Curriculum of Mathematics as Secondary Level

After selecting the topics curriculum has to be organized maintaining the mathematical sequence and continuity.

## Principles of Curriculum Organization

The arrangement of topics in each class should be guided by the students ability to grasp assimilate, retain and apply the mathematical concepts at a particular age level. The focus should be on the students and its capabilities rather than on the amount of information to be presented. The arrangement should be from concrete to abstract. The following principals should be kept in mind while organizing mathematics curriculum.

## Principles of correlation

While organizing the content in mathematics curriculum the principles of correlation should be followed. The following four types of correlation should be considered.

(*i*) Correlation with life.

(*ii*) Correlation with other subjects.

(*iii*) Correlation between different branches of mathematics

(*iv*) Correlation between different topics in the same branch of the mathematics.

## Principle of Logical & Psychological orders

An Integrated approach combining both logical & psychological orders should be followed in the organization of the mathematics curriculum. It should display sequential development of topics which is almost appropriate for the student of that age level.

## Principle of activity

Learning by doing makes learning more meaningful. The curriculum organization should take into consideration the types of activities that could be provided for the effectives learning of the content. The activities include

- Personal & home activities.
- Vocational activities.
- Recreational activities.

- National activities.
- Community, civic and social activities.

**The Criterion of Difficulty**

The organization o the content should in the increasing order of difficulty. The difficulty level of topics is to be judged from the students points of view, based on the mental development and capabilities of the students.

**Application to Individual differences**

The arrangement of the content for each class and level should cater to the needs of different categories of children. There should be topics which are challenging for mathematically gifted students and topics suitable for average and slow learners in mathematics. Similarly needs of students from rural and urban areas and from different communities have to be given due weightage while arranging the mathematics curriculum.

### 1.3.2 Concepts of Syllabus

The syllabus is defined as the documents that consist of topics or portion covered in a particular subject. It is determined by the examination board and created by the experienced teachers. Members of syllabus creation committee are responsible for the quality of the course. Syllabus is considered as guide to the incharge as well as to the student.

Syllabus means teaching experience which is to be given in classroom for completing some objective of curriculum in specific period. Division wise topic of curriculum is also called as syllabus.

- **Method of Construction of Curriculum in Mathematics :-**

### 1.3.3 Concentric / Spiral Method

The Cambridge report ( 1963) on mathematics curriculum emphasised the importance of interelating and interweaving the different mathematical topic to be taken up throughout broadening and deepening of the students mathematical knowledge and insight by what is called the 'Spiral Method'.

In Spiral method topics are divided into a number of smaller independent units to be dealt with in order of difficulty suiting the, mental capabilities of children. In this method, elementary concepts are presented in one class gaps are filled in the next class, and more gaps in a year or two later in accordance with the amount of knowledge which the student are capable of assimilating.

Titles, units, even teaching subject also remains in this method only its scope increases in each division. Knowledge of previous units helps student for understanding of new topic. Teacher also gets helps of knowledge of previous units of students to increase their curiosity for learning of new topics nature of this method is just like drawing a various circle of different radius having one centre so this method is also called as Concentric method.

This method implies widening of knowledge just as concentric circles go on extending and widening. The study of topic is spread over a number of years. Beginning from nucleus the circles of Knowledge goes on widening year after year.

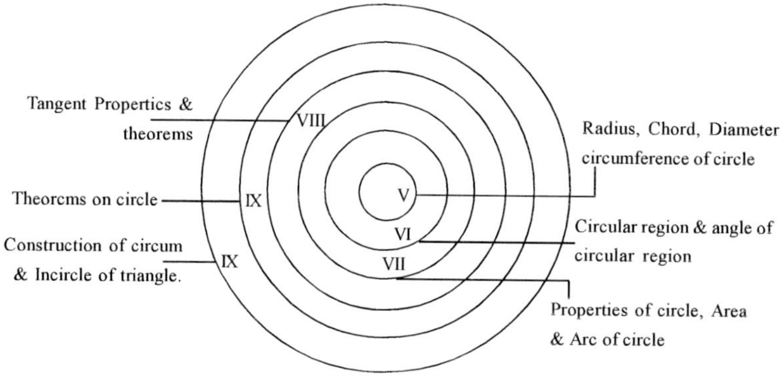


**Figure 1.3**

An elementary knowledge is given in the introductory year, something more is taught in the year, something still more is added in the subsequent year and so on. A steady progress is maintained in the acquisition knowledge of a topic for a sufficient numbers of years continuously.

A topic is broken into a number of portion and the portions are allotted to various classes. The criteria are difficulty of Portions and power of comprehension of student in an age group. Any gaps of knowledge are filled up year after year fully fledged knowledge of the topic is ultimately provided. It is mostly Concerned with year to year teaching but it influence can be exercised in day to day teaching well. Knowledge to be given today should follow from the knowledge given on previous day and should lead to the teaching on the following days.

**Merits of Concentric Method**

1. It is suitable system of arrangement because its opposite is highly unpsychological.
2. It enables the teacher to do a portion of a topic according to the receptively of learners. The learners get as much as they can grasp.
3 Continuance of the study of a topic for a number of years makes its impression more lasting.
4. Previous Knowledge or comprehension of a topic is revised year after year which helps in its retention.
5 It does not allow the teaching to become dull. The Interest of the student remains alive for the short duration of a topic every year a new Interest can be created for the topic.

**Demerits**

1. If a portion is too long the interest is likely to flag; and if portion is too short it is not likely to make any lasting or permanent impression on the learners mind.
2 It may prove harmful, If a teacher becomes over ambitious and exhausts all the possible interesting illustrations in the introductory year.

## Linear Method

Method of Introducing particular topic or portion the syllabus of Specific division in curriculum construction Process is called as liner method.

In mathematics topic like Post transaction, Commission, Share Market, Simple Interest, Compound Interest. Bill & receipts have limited scope their teaching content can be taught in one or two unit. By considering students age topics can be introduced for one division in curriculum construction process. No need remains to extend it to next division such topics or their content comes not in use as a preknowledge at the time of teaching of other units of mathematics.

While units like area, volume, types of equations (liner, simultaneous, quadratic) Geometric construction can be not completed in one or two chapters or in division syllabus of two or more divisions according to their Scope in Curriculum Construction process topics have same titles for different division syllabus but there is difference in content of Previous and next division syllabus. In Concentric Method depth of topic or portion increases as per divisions but this not occur in linear method.

e.g. Area, dimensions, needs dimensions area of various geometrical diagrams, Areas of irregular diagram is the topic. In the syllabus of 6th div unit area, area of rectangle

square and dimension is included while area of equilateral triangle; Parallelogram and trapezium is included in the syllabus of 7th and for 8th units like area of quadrilateral, irregular diagram circle are included then this example of liner method in Curriculum construction.

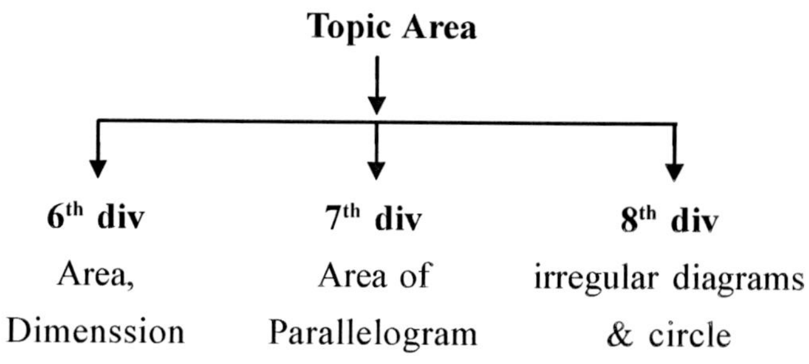

It is opposite of concentric method concentric method involves the breaking up of topic into suitable Portion whereas aims at keeping it intact. A topic is taken as a unified whole or as an unbreakable unit. It is based on the principle that any topic when begun should not be left half done. It should be finished in its entirety, before the next topic is taken.

### Merits of Linear Method

1. Continuous teaching of a topic not only will save the students from divided concentration, but may ensure their full and whole hearted Concentration on the topic in hand also.

2 A natural link and sequence will exist in the day to day work in class room.

3. The student complete attention, ability and capacity will be directed exclusively to the topic under study for a sufficiently long time.

4 When a topic is treated as center for other topics it facilitates the learning process. It illustrate it the advantage of correlation.

### Drawbacks of Linear Method

1 Keeping psychological reasons in view, it will be foolish to take up a topic like area in lower classes and try to finish it at stretch.

2. In this method a topic takes much time to be completed, so only few topics will find place in the syllabus of a particular class.

3 Linear method does not provide any opportunity for year to year revision.

4. Most of the knowledge acquired in earlier year is likely to be forgotten by the time the student leave the school.

### 1.3.4 Difference between Syllabus & Curriculum

| | CURRICULUM | SYLLABUS |
|---|---|---|
| 1. | Curriculum refers to the overall content taught in an educational system or in a course. | Syllabus is described as the summery of the topic Covered or Units to be taught in the particular subject. |
| 2. | The term Curriculum has a Latin Origin. | The term syllabus have a Greek Origin |
| 3. | Curriculum in a wider concept. | Syllabus is a limited part of Curriculum. |
| 4. | Curriculum in not made available to student unless specially asked for. | Syllabus is provided to the student by committee of Expert and experience teacher. |
| 5. | Curriculum is Prescriptive in nature. | Syllabus is descriptive in nature. |
| 6. | Curriculum Covers a Particular Course of Study of Program. | Syllabus is set for particular subject |
| 7. | Duration of Curriculum is lasts till the Completion of the course. | Duration of a syllabus is for a year only |
| 8. | Curriculum is created for difference level like Primary Secondary & Higher Secondary. | Syllabus is prepared for a particularly each division |

## 1.4 TEXT BOOK OF MATHEMATICS

### 1.4.1 Place of Text Book

Text book play a important role in the present days teaching and learning of mathematics. What is to be taught and learnt in a particular class is entirely based on the prescribed text book of mathematics for that class. The text book helps the teacher for his teaching, for the student his learning and for the examiner his examining task. There is nothing beyond the text book which is taught and learnt. In this way the teacher, the tutor and the examination system all have become slaves in the hands of the text book.

This type of slowery has been responsible for the deteriorating conditions in teaching of mathematics. The students have become book worms. If a little care is taken in the selection of proper text book and if they are used in a proper way, there is no doubt that the text book would delinatly prove quite useful and helping hand to the teacher and the student.

The usefulness of such text book in the teaching of mathematics can be seen through the following points.

### Need of text book in teaching of mathematics

#### A Usefulness to the teachers

(*i*) In a text book, the relevant matter concerning the syllabus of that class is readily available. Therefore text book guide the teacher about the boundaries and limits of his teaching in a particular class.

(*ii*) Valuable knowledge and information collected from various sources is readily available in a text book. More ever this information is presented in a well organized & systematic from.

(*iii*) Text books are usually written by the well experienced teachers and subject experts. A teacher can make use of their services by making use of their text books.

(*iv*) Text book help the teacher in planning his lessons, deciding his method of teaching & preparing suitable aids.

(*v*) Text book of mathematics presents illustrative example concerning various type of problems are readily available and thus the teacher has not bother himself for the setting of syllabus and problems.

(*vi*) The task of playing individual attention of the student becomes quite simple to the teachers by making use of text book in mathematics.

#### B Usefulness for the student

(*i*) Through text book, student becomes acquainted with what is to be studied in a particulars class. Such clarity of aims and objectives helps in maintaining the desired interest in the study.

(*ii*) Text book help in preparation at their home. Students may get themselves prepared for studying the next day lesson.

(*iii*) Text book save time and energy of the student. They not copy the illustrative examples or problems written on the black- board. In writing do problems and question for drill and home work. They are again saved from unnecessary labour.

(*iv*) Sometimes students do mistakes in copying the formulae, symbols, definition and principles from the black board of other times there remain gaps due to their inability of quick understanding or slow writing under these situations text book help a lot in supplementing as well as correcting class notes.

(*v*) In class rooms it becomes difficult to cater to the needs of all types of students. Text books help in this direction by meeting the requirement of the slow, average and fast learner.

(*vi*) Text book help in doing self-study and helping the students to acquire the habit of independent learning.

**Characteristic of a model text book in mathematics**

- Text book should be strictly written according to the prescribed syllabus. It should properly and evently attend each and every aspect of the syllabus.
- It should be according to the aims and objectives of teaching mathematics in that particular class.
- It should meet the abilities, experience and interest of that student for which it has been written. It should cater to the needs of all types of student slow, average and fast learners.
- The day to day needs of the students & their physical and social environment should find due place in the text book.
- The text book should be written according to the demands of Modern Mathematics. The units of weights and measurement and coinage should be in metric system.
- The psychological as well as logical order should be followed in the organization of the subject matter of the text-book.

- The principle ' Simple to Complex' should be followed in the arrangement of the topics of the text-book.
- The subject matter should be organized on the principle of concentric order so that what is being taught may be correlated with the part and future learning.
- All the definitions, concept & principle given in the text book should be as clear and definite as possible.
- The illustrative example given in the text book should be quite appropriate. They should neither be too much nor too less in number.
- It should contain provision for the revision of the work done in the previous class.
- The presentation of the subject matter must be as attractive and interesting as possible. The illustration in terms of picture, figure and diagram should be quite appropriate.
- The principle of 'learning by doing' and from 'concrete to abstract' should be properly followed for illustration of the subject matter.
- The language of the problems should be quite simple and clear interesting & purposeful.
- The paper used in the text book should be of superior quality. It should also have quality printing and the binding of the text book should be durable.
- 'The book should specifically mention the date of first copy right edition should current with necessary modifications.
- It should be moderately priced & readily available in the market.

**Essential of a Good Text-Book**

- It should have the necessary external qualities i.e. it's get up, paper & printing etc. should be good.
- In spite of various qualities, it should be moderately priced.

- It should be free from mistake & the style should be straight forward. In a mathematical text-book even the most ordinary printing mistake can play havoc.
- To avoid spoon feeding, there should not be too many solved example. The student should get adequate opportunity of learning through initiative and independent efforts.
- It should be up to date as regards the subject matter.
- There should be sufficient provision for practice and review. It should meet demand of student in ability and interest.
- There should not be irrelevant matter.
- It should satisfy the demands of examination also.
- It should be easily available in the market.

### 1.4.2 Text Book Analysis

S tudent of secondary schools handles mathematics books for two or three times per day. He has to carry it in school each day. Though Educationalist and Psychologist are expressed their opinion regarding to reduce load of books and notebooks from students back; student has to bring mathematics books daily to school. By considering the daily use of mathematics books it should be light to weight and easy to understand at the time of study.

Each new book always analyzed by teachers, experienced teachers, educationalist, Journalist. At the time of analysis of mathematics following points are considered.

A mathematics book is analyzed by two aspects; one is internal and another is external aspects.

**Points for analysis of internal aspects of Mathematics book**

(*i*)Index

(*ii*) Organization of Subject and Topics

(*iii*) Pictures & illustrations

(*iv*) Formulae & Principles

(*v*) Language
(*vi*) Vocabulary & linguistic items
(*vii*) Introduction of each new topic
(*viii*) Use of teaching of maxims
(*ix*) Glossary
(*x*) Exercise, Activities, Projects and Practical's

**Points for analysis of internal aspects of Mathematics book**

(*i*) Front Cover
(*ii*) Back Cover
(*iii*) Paper Quality
(*iv*) Price
(*v*) Binding
(*vi*) Size of the Text Books
(*vii*) Font size of Text, Formulae, Principle and law
(*viii*) Charts, Diagrams and graphs
(*ix*) Preface
(*x*) Printing

Explanation of Points for analysis of internal aspects of Mathematics book-

**Index**

A good Index has headings and subheadings that are concise and reflecting the content used in the text. It also has enough cross references to connect related terms, proper alphabetization and page references. A good index reveals the interrelationships of topics, concepts and names so that the students need not read the whole index to find what they are looking for.

**Organization of Subject and topics**

The organization of the content should be simple. It has to be organized in a logical and understandable manner. The book should cover topics which are relevant, useful and serves the purpose of the book. Each topic should be covered comprehensively.

**Pictures and illustration**

The Pictures and illustrations should be relevant to the content and properly distributed throughout the text book. The pictures should be well drawn and realistic. There should be appropriateness and vividness in pictures and illustrations and they should develop interest and motivate learners. Actually mathematics book contains more geometrical diagrams than pictures. In Geometrical constructions topic sampling diagram are not with real measurements so there should be proper explanation regarding this.

**Formulae and Principles**

It has been said that, "If we have to go in the forest of mathematics then we should have gun of formulae." This sentence explains importance of formulae in mathematics. So it is necessary that formulae and principles should not be directly given in any topic of mathematics. They should be derived and explained with the help of examples in books. Due to this pattern it gets easy to remember formulae for long time and even they can prepare formulae after forgetting.

They should be in bold and framed on the pages in each book of mathematics. Even at the end of topic, means, in summary formulae and principal should be once again reviewed serially.

**Language**

Already 50% student's perception regarding the subject mathematics is that it is a hard subject. Every student has to handle mathematics book at least one time per day. The language of text should be simple and in accordance with the mental level of learners. The language should be appropriate to the situation on content and free from error and mistakes.

**Introduction of each new topic**

According to sentence, 'Well begun is half done'; if introduction of each new topic in the book of mathematics is succeeded to create interest and sustain curiosity then it will be very useful for each learner. Introduction of each topic should start with information or questioning on preknowledge related to new topic. If topic is completely new then it should have proper information due to which student will show eagerness for learning the same.

**Use of Maxims of teaching**

The subject should be properly organized and graded in order of difficulty. The content should follow maxims of teaching. i.e. from simple to complex, from known to unknown, from specific to general, from general to specific etc.

**Glossary**

A glossary should include terms which are newly introduced, unknown and specialized. Each new words, formulae and expressions should be defined and explained properly.

**Exercise, Activities, projects and Practicals**

There should be sufficient numbers of exercise and activities to provide better scope of learning for all the learners. Exercise should be properly graded, purposeful and adequate. Instructions to do exercise, activities, projects and practicals should be clear and precise. It should also satisfy demand of examination and should have comprehensiveness and utility.

**Explanation of Points for analysis of External aspects of Mathematics book**

**Front & Back Page cover**

Look of the front & back page cover of mathematics text book should be of the such type that student get attracted to it readily after seeing. This means that on front and back page picture or matter should reflect soul of total content of that book. Student or anyone who is handling for the first time should get idea regarding knowledge of the book. In short it should be colorful, attractive and appropriate. It should be durable and reflect the content of the syllabus.

### Paper Quality

The Paper used should be reasonable and of good quality. It should be adequately thick, durable and smooth. It should be bright and clear in appearance.

### Price

The price should be reasonable and in accordance to the content and demand of the book. It should be affordable to majority of the parents.

### Binding

Students use mathematics text book frequently in school everyday and also for doing exercise at home. So, the binding of the book should be sufficiently strong as considering the handling of the text book of mathematics by the student each day.

### Size of the text book

Size of the textbook should be in accordance with the age group of the students. The number of the pages should be appropriately balanced with the required content. It should not be too heavy to carry.

### Font size of the content

The font size should be suitable for the age group. A balance in the use of different font size should be maintained and it should not strain the eyesight of the pupils.

### Charts, Diagrams and graphs

There should be reality, adoptiveness and vividness in charts, diagrams and graphs. Diagram and chart should be accurate, clear, well drawn. It should develop interest. Size of charts, diagrams and graphs should be suitable for the age group. It should be colorful for lower level students.

### Preface

Preface is an introduction to a book. It should include information about the book. A preface should give brief description, the characteristic or theme and should state purpose of the book. It should give just enough to get the reader interested in reading the book.

**Printing**

The printing should be neat and clean. The spacing between words, line and paragraph should be even. Printing should be free from any type of error.

### 1.4.3 Content Analysis of Mathematics

Mathematics means not only the skill of Arithmetic and calculation; it is a structure. Structure means logical arrangement of knowledge which can be achieved through scientifical frame. Mathematics is a subject of man made logical thoughts. It has a special language in which signs, symbols, mathematical concepts like Set, Prime numbers, similarity and functions are basic units of mathematical language. For development of mathematical language it is necessary to understand relationship between basic concepts.

Arithmetic, Algebra, Geometry are three branches of mathematics at secondary level. Arithmetic is mathematics of numbers in which addition, subtraction, multiplication and division basic process are used. Study of odd, even, triangular and quadrilateral numbers is also part of it. Algebra is developed on basis of arithmetic in which numbers and words are both used. Algebra is compact language as its arithmetic relation with algebra. It has also relation with geometry. Some geometric problems are solved with the help of algebra. Up to this we are well familiar that arithmetic is a science of numbers, algebra is of words and geometry is of volume. Geometry is self contained structure of deductive thought. Its nature has become imaginary from the measurement of land with the help of indefinable word, definition, axioms. Some statement can be proved by using logic. Major concepts of geometry are imaginary. It is inclusion of axioms, theorems, pre theorems and sub theorems.

We have seen compact nature of mathematics; we have now to understand that mathematics is subject with special content. Its content has various topics. Interrelationship to analyze topic and to find out Interrelation among it, means content analysis.

Explanation of word 'Content analysis' in the words of I. K. Davis, "It is the analysis of topic or content unit to be taught into its constituents or elements and arrange them in logical sequence". Content analysis is the most important activity for teacher. Through content analysis a detailed study has to be completed by a teacher. It results in a minute study of content. Teacher may think about the objectives which can be taught in his subject and which particular content teacher is going to teach.

Teacher can select a proper teaching method according to the nature of content by considering student ability.

## Need and Importance of Content analysis

When teacher thinks about teaching of new topic of mathematics of secondary level; first they have to take review whether the student had already learnt related to new teaching topic in current or previous standard. Due to which he gets guidelines for starting the teaching of topic means for introduction. Then he has to prepare the list of teaching point. After preparing the list of teaching point he thinks on teaching method, teaching models and teaching point. For teaching the new topic there is need of preparing teaching points, upto what extent this topic should be taught? For this and more teacher needs to do content analysis.

## Importance of Content analysis

(*i*) Teacher gets information about teaching points.

(*ii*) Teacher can select a proper teaching method according to the nature of content.

(*iii*) To select knowledge representative according to the content.

(*iv*) To decide evaluation tool, content analysis is very important.

(*v*) Teacher gets information about upto what extent topic is to teach.

(*vi*) Teacher can alerts student how this unit is useful in future.

### 1.4.4 Categories of Content Analysis

1. Content analysis by Davis technique.
2. Content analysis by Evaluation technique
3. Content's cognitive psychological analysis

Here we are discussing first two techniques:

## CONTENT ANALYSIS BY DAVIS TECHNIQUE

In Davis technique which content we used to teach is analyzed with main and sub points as per logical sequence or order to teach. So Davis defined content analysis, "content analysis means logical and sequential order of main & sub points of selected topic.

**For example** - we have to teach the unit 'set 'to 9th standard of algebra. Its content analysis will be as follow -

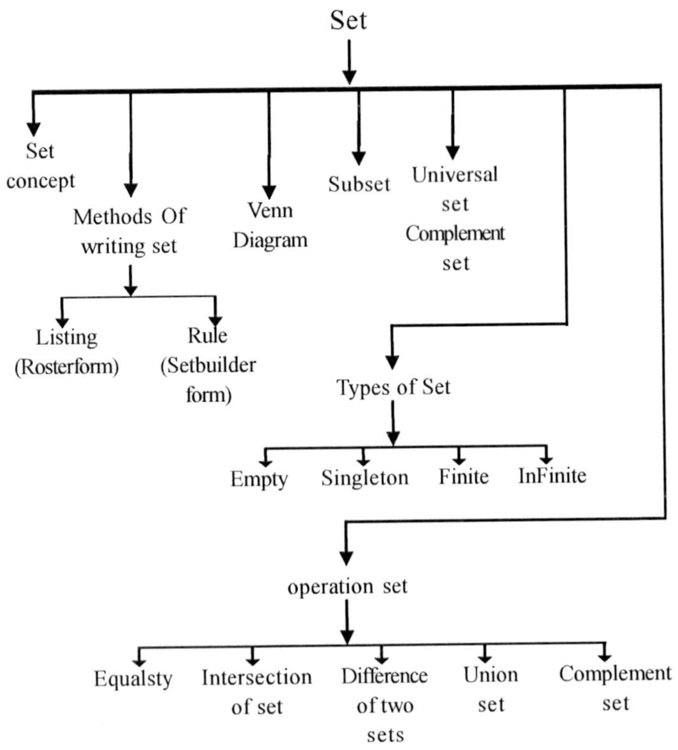

**Evaluation technique**

This technique comes into focus after arrival of Dr. B.J. Bloom evaluation approach. In personality development; cognitive, emotional and psychometric domain is considered. Dr.Bloom has constituted a hierarchy of three types of domain. Currently we use these three domains for finalizing objectives and content analysis. These three domains are also useful for content analysis. From these three domains we are thinking content analysis according to cognitive domain.

Following component is always getting to see in various subject contents but it is not possible that every component will get included in each topic content.

1. Term - Name of any concrete or abstract thing. teaching -learning of Terms is upto knowledge level. In the teaching of terms like point, line, linear-nonlinear points, parallel line, segment, circle, angle, meaning of them to understand to student is expected.
2. Concepts- Name of groups or group of concrete or abstract thing having common characteristic.

   **e.g. :-** Triangle, quadrilateral, indices.
3. Principle- principle means statement which shows relationship between two or more concepts.
4. Law - Systematic collection of various principles.

   **e.g. :-** laws of Indices- $a^m$ x $a^n$= $a^{m+n}$
5. Fact - fact is defined as form of data which is singular in accuracy, happens in a past or poor or present and has no predictive value (Bruner)

   **e.g.:-** Statement giving answer of the question like 'What is this?'Is fact.

   We can't predict from fact but it is useful for taking decisions.

   **e.g.:** i) AB is a line. ii) 7+2=9

1 Signs- an object, quality or event whose presence or occurrence indicates the probable presence or occurrence of something else.

**e.g. :-** +, -, x, -=-, =, <, >,@,p,~

**7.** Formula-A set of symbols expressing a mathematical rule, law or principle.

E.g. Area of rectangle = A(A) = l×B

l = length & b= breadth

**8.** Theory - An idea or set of ideas that is intended to explain facts or events.

Theory means an idea or a statement made by a studious person stated with the deep study or by making some experiments which can be tested or prove the facts.

**e.g.:-** if i) **e.g.:–** if i) $\frac{a}{b} = \frac{c}{d}$, then $\frac{a}{b} = \frac{a+c}{b+d} = \frac{c}{d}$

ii) $Sin^2A + cos^2A = 1$

**9.** Proof - Process of establishing the conclusion by logical reasoning on the basis of axioms and previously proved theorems.

**10.** Definition - Definition is the statement of the meaning of a term (a word, phrase, or other set of symbols). Definitions are given in two types i.e. in Descriptive or Operational form.

**11.** Characteristic - A feature or quality belonging typically to a person, place, objects or abstract thing and serving to identify them.

**e.g.:-** *i*) Characteristic of triangle

(*ii*) Characteristic of polygon Skill of geometric construction

**12.** Structure - The arrangement of and relationship between the parts or elements of something complex structure of mathematics.

**13.** Skill - ability and capacity acquired through deliberate, systematic, and sustained effort to smoothly and adaptively carry out complex activities.

For example - *i*) skill of calculation

(*ii*) Skill of Geometrical construction

**14.** Pretheorem - Before proving theorem, complementary statement is already proved and it is useful for the proof of a theorem

For example- The measure of an exterior angle of triangle is equal to sum of measures of its remote interior angle.

**15.** Axioms - Statement accepted by mathematician or statement accepted without proof.

In another way axioms are defined as the terms of statements whose proof are not to be asked are called axioms.

**16.** Theorems- Statement that we prove from axioms is called as theorems. In this way we studied component which are to be taken into consideration in mathematics content analysis.

**Sample of content analysis as per evaluation technique is as follow**

**Sub - Geometry** **Std.- 9 th**

**Unit No. -1 : Lines and angles**

| No. | Content Component. | Nature of Content. |
|---|---|---|
| 1 | Terms | Collinear& NonCollinear pts., Planes, Betweeness, angle, zero & straight angle. |
| 2 | Concepts | Parallel lines, Betweeness, Segment, and ray, Congruent Segment & Opposite ray angle. |
| 3 | Definition | Collinear&Noncollinearpts., Measures of angles, Directed angle & Reflex angle |
| 4 | Diagram | Plane, Congruent Segment, angle(zero, Directed & Reflex angle) |
| 5 | Properties | Congruent segment, Congruent angle |

# Chapter-2

# PEDAGOGICAL APPROACHES & RESOURCES OF MATHEMATICS

## 2.1 METHOD OF TEACHING MATHEMATICS

A mathematics teacher has a variety of method and techniques available for use in teaching mathematics. The selection of suitable method depends upon the objectives of the lesson, needs of the learner and the nature of the content.

Some methods are more appropriate for teaching students as a group whereas some are specially designed for individualized instruction. Following methods are discussed in this chapter

1. Demonstration
2. Lecture Demonstration
3. Inductive - Deductive
4. Analytic- Synthetic
5. Experiment-
6. Heuristic
7. Project

### 2.1.1 Demonstration Method

In the mathematics teaching demonstration method is very important. In this method both the teacher and pupil are active. The teacher makes a theoretical investigation and proves it in the class room. The teacher performs the experiment while teaching in the class and the pupils acquire knowledge with careful observation of the experiment. Demonstration may be performed by a single teacher or a group of teacher. The teacher should emphasize major points in the demonstrations and preferably should write them on black board. The teacher should be well-versed in the handling of the apparatus and equipments while demonstrating teacher should ask some reflective type of question to stimulate the power of reasoning and interest of should in the classroom.

**Example**:-If teacher wants to teach various type of polygons and their classification in the class.

**Solution:** -The procedure to teach this topic may be as follows-
The teacher will show 3, 4, 5, 6, sided closed figures

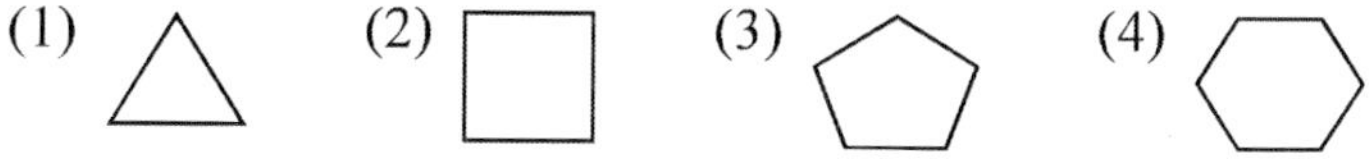


**Question & Answer**

1. How many sides does each of the figures have?

   Ans. → The pupil will identify the number of sides in each figure.

2. How sides may does have fig.(1)?

   Ans. → Three.

3. What is the name of this figure?

   Ans. → Triangle.

4. How many sides do have the fig. (2)?

   Ans. → Four.

5 What is the name of figure?

   Ans. → Quadrilateral.

6. How sides may does have the fig.(3)?

   Ans. → Five.

   (Teacher gives name of figure having side 5 is pentagon)

7. How many sides do have the fig.(4)?

   Ans. → Six.

8. What is the name of the figure?

   Ans. → Hexagon

   Teacher says that the common name of all these figure is 'polygon'

**9.** Can you define 'Polygon'

Ans. → Student thinks and tries to give answer

Teacher finally states the definition

Polygon - is a simple closed plane figure formed by live segments e.g. Triangle, Quadrilateral etc.

**10.** What is the basis of classification of 'Polygon'?

Student answers as per their view, then teacher explains expected answers.

Polygons are classified on the basis of numbers of sides they have, the teacher shows a chart illustrating the various polygons of different sides & their names as follows.

**Different kinds of 'Polygon'**

| | | |
|---|---|---|
| 1. | 3 sides - Triangle |  |
| 2. | 4 sides - Quadrilateral |  |
| 3. | 5 sides - Pentagon |  |
| 4. | 6 sides - Hexagon |  |
| 5. | 7 sides - Heptagon |  |
| 6. | 8 sides - Octagon |  |
| 7. | 9 sides - Nonagon |  |
| 8. | 10 sides - Decagon |  |

**Precautions or criteria of a Good Demonstration**

1. The purpose of demonstration should be stated before the students clearly.
2. All experiments should be performed in front of the children.
3. The demonstration table should be arranged properly so that all pupils are able to see it properly. The demonstration should be at higher level.
4. The help of student should be taken while demonstration.
5. Doubts of pupils should be cleared simultaneously.

6. The teacher should use easy and simple language.
7. After the completion of demonstration the teacher should discuss the observation and result of the demonstration.
8. Demonstration should be supplemented with the other Audio visual aids to make it more interesting and effective.

**Merits**

1. The teaching becomes effectives even if the numbers of apparatus are less.
2. The pupil develops the powers of observation, reasoning and thinking.
3. Demonstration method is appropriate for lower classes.
4. Students learn by seeing and observing.
5. It is economical method.
6. Students can understand the principles/ law/ formulae clearly.
7. It is useful where the experiments involve some complex and difficult operations.
8. It is more useful where the apparatus is costly and sensitive to break.

**Demerits**

1. The pupils do not get a chance to perform experiments. Therefore firsthand experience is not possible with the use of this method.
2. It is not based on the principle learning by doing.
3. The pupils only observe, what the teacher 'does'.
4. The pupils do not get direct experiences.

### 2.1.2 Lecture Demonstration

Lecture Demonstration method is considered to be a method superior to lecture method as it combines the advantages of both lecture and the demonstration method.

This method can be effectively used for teachings mathematics. By using this method it is possible to easily impart concrete experience to student during the course of lesson, when the teacher's wants to explain some abstract points. This method combines the instructional strategy' Information imparting and showing how' for example, while teaching geometrical constructions the teacher has to explain how to construct the geometrical figure with the given specification simultaneously demonstrating how to carry out the construction following the sequence of steps.

In this method the teacher performs the experiment before the class and simultaneously explains what he is doing. For example while Explaining how to form a right circular hollow cone using a sector cutout from a circle, the teacher has to show how to fold sector to get a cone so that the radius of the sector becomes the slant height of the cone. He also encourages student participation by asking relevant question, requiring them to keenly observe and draw inferences. Afterwards through questioning and cross questioning the interferences drawn by the students are discussed in the class.

### Merits of Lecture-Demonstration Method

- It is a psychological method as students take active interest in the learning process.
- It is useful for all students of varying abilities.
- It is an economical method as compared to purely student centered method.
- It leads the student from concrete experiences to abstract concept.
- It encourages student participation in learning.
- It trains mental faculties such as power of observation, reasoning, and drawing inferences.

### Demerits of Lecture-Demonstration Method

- It does not provide firsthand experience to the student.
- It does not provide for Individual difference. It caters to the needs of average student.
- It does not develop manual and manipulative skill and cannot be substitute for laboratory method.
- It is not applicable for higher level mathematics.

**Applicability of Lecture - Demonstration Method**

Lecture - Demonstration method is best suitable for teaching mathematics at lower classes. All topics in mathematics do not yield for the use of this method. Construction of geometrical figures & same basic concepts in geometry can be most effectively taught through lecture-demonstration.

## 2.1.3 Experimental Method

Experimental method is procedure for stimulating the activities of the students & to encourage them to make discoveries. In this method student require to do some experiments or carry out certain activities in order to verity the validity of mathematical generalization portion of the Inductive method or the practical form of heuristic method. Therefore, in this method he proceed from concrete to abstract. It is based on the psychological principles of learning such as 'learning by doing', 'learning by observation' & so on. Method is quite competent to relate the theoretical knowledge with the practical base. This approach makes the learning process more interesting lively and meaningful.

The success of the experimental method depends on the able and skilled mathematics teacher as well as the availability of a well equipped mathematics laboratory. This method can easily be applied in a class room and also out of classroom. In words of J.W.A. Young, "The Experimental method aims to arouse teachers to a belief, not only theoretical but practical and effective as well, that mathematical dishes must be made appetizing and palatable. They are to be accepted with pleasure and digested with ease."

Essential equipments for Experiments of mathematics -

Experimental method can be used successfully, if there is a well equipped laboratory of mathematical Instruments and other teaching aids. The following are some essential equipments and teaching aids for a laboratory of mathematics.

1. Geometrical Instruments
2. Mathematical models of geometrical solids as cube, cuboid, sphere, cone, prism, cylinder etc.

3. Charts, maps, graph papers, flash board, drawing papers etc.
4. Balance, measuring tape, weights, calculating machine, angle mirror, dividers, lever, pulley, cardboard, meter-scale, scissors etc.
5. Films, slides, screen projector etc.
6. Logarithmic tables, slide rule, etc.
7. Books and magazines related to mathematics
8. Other essential teaching aids and well seating arrangement.

**Procedure of Experimental Method**

There are no general specified steps to be followed in the use of this method. The teacher and students have to proceed according to the need of the problem and experiment.

The following examples illustrate the use of this method.

**Example 1**

**Topic or the Problem-** To find the formula for the area of a rectangle

**Material aids-** Graph Paper, Pencil, scale, drawing board, pins etc.

**Formula used-** The total number of unit squares lying within the figure of rectangle is the area of the rectangle.

**Procedure -** Fix a graph paper on the drawing board with the help of board pins. Draw the figure of a rectangle of specific length and breadth. Now count the squares of graph lying within the figure of rectangle. Write your observations and findings on a plain paper or in a note book. Now draw another rectangle of different length and breadth on a graph paper and again count the squares lying within the figure of the rectangle. Write those observation and findings in the observation table of your note book. This procedure should be repeated by drawing four-five rectangles of different lengths and breadths. The findings regarding area of different rectangle should be noted in the observation table as given.

OBSERVATION TABLE

| No. | Measurement of rectangles | | Total numbers of unit squares lying within the figure of rectangle on the graph paper | Area of Rectangle |
|---|---|---|---|---|
| | Length × | Breadth | | |
| 1 | 5 cms. | 4 cms. | 20 square of 1 sq.cms. | 20 sq.cms. |
| 2 | 8 cms. | 4 cms. | 32 square of 1 sq.cms. | 32 sq.cms. |
| 3 | 10 cms. | 6 cms. | 60 square of 1 sq.cms. | 60 sq.cms. |
| 4 | 7 cms. | 5 cms. | 35 square of 1 sq.cms. | 35 sq.cms. |
| 5 | 3 cms. | 2 cms. | 6 square of 1 sq.cms. | 6 sq.cms. |

## Analysis of observed data

After preparing observation table, its data should be analyzed to reach on certain conclusion. From the above observation table we can easily analyze that in each observation the area of rectangle is equal to the product of its length and breadth.

## Conclusion or Inference

The area of rectangle is the product of length and breadth. Therefore, in the form of formula it can be written as Area of rectangle = length × breadth

## Merits

1 It is based on the psychological laws of learning law of exercise and law of effect.

2. It is based on the principle of learning by doing.

3. It stimulates the interest of the students to work with concrete material.

4 It provides an opportunity for the student to verify the validity of the mathematics rules through their application.

5. Knowledge and skill acquired though experiments helps in better understanding and longer retention.

6 It promotes self-confidence and self reliance and a sense of achievement among the students.

7 It provides opportunities for social interaction and cooperation among the students.

8 It develops habits of scientific enquiry and Investigation.

**Demerits**

1. Experimental method does not contribute much towards the method development of the students.
2. It is an expensive method in terms of time, equipment, laboratory, facilities and number of skilled and able teacher's.
3. Only few topics in mathematics can be taught through this method and hence it has limited applicability.
4. It is too much to expect the students to work independently and discover and verify mathematics facts like mathematical.

5 It is not suitable for larger classes as the teacher has to give individual attention to each student.

6. It is suitable for only lower classes.

**Applicability of Experimental Method**

Experimental method is best suited for teaching mathematics at lower classes; this method does not provide much scope for teaching mathematics at high school and higher secondary classes. However many topics in geometry, measuration and applied mathematics can be taught effectively though experimental method.

**Some Sample Topics for Experimental Method**

**Derivation of the formulae for the:-**

(*i*) Circumference of a circle, area of a circle.

(*ii*) Area of square, rectangle, parallelogram and trapezium.

(*iii*) Area of triangle, right angled triangle, isosceles right angle triangle.

(*iv*) Total surface area of cone, cylinder.

(*v*) Volume of a sphere.

(*vi*) Volume of cone.

1. Expansion of identities as

   $(a+b)^2$; $(a-b)^2$; $(a+b+c)^2$; (a+b) x (a-b); $(a+b)^3$

2. Verification of

   (*i*) Properties of certain Geometric figure like parallelogram, rhombus.

   (*ii*) Transversal Properties.

   (*iii*) Properties of vertically opposite angles formed by interesting lines.

   (*iv*) Congruency postulates.

   (*v*) Theorems relating to triangles and circulars.

### 2.1.4 Heuristic Method

Like other method Heuristic method also has a special place in mathematics teaching. The world heuristic is believed to be originated from Greek world "Heuristic" which means "I find out". the profounder of this method is Prof. Armstrong.

This method is more important from educational point of view because in this method student work like a researcher and solve the problem. By the use of this method scientific and mathematical attitude can be developed in students. Herbert Spencer has thrown high on this method and stated that "Student should be told minimum and as much as possible they should be encouraged to discover"

This method was developed and perfected by Prof Henry Edward Armstrong According to him "Heuristic method is the method of teaching which places the student as far as possible in the attitude discovery". He accepted the principle of teaching given by Herbert Spencer that "children should be told as little as possible and induced to discover as much as possible" as main basis for this method. He was of the opinion that the school should develop thinking power of the child and for this latter must be given an opportunity to think. This method has also been found useful in teaching of mathematics. Here primary consideration is the development of thinking power self confidence, originality and self judgment in the child to make him

and ever successful people rather than acquirement of informative knowledge. Thus it aims at training a learner in the method of learning. It imparts a sound training in educational of self.

**Example :-** The population of the city is so over. If percentage increase in population is 4% per year then find out the population of the city after 2 Year.

**Solution :-** Teacher will tell the students to repeat this question many time and will tell them to find the solution with the help of suitable researching question and he will encourage them for finding correct solution. We can understand the solution of the problem with the help of question asked by the teacher.

The question asked by the teacher and expected answers given by the students are listed in the following table.

| No. | Question asked by Teacher | Expected answer given by Student |
|---|---|---|
| 1. | What has to be calculated in the given question? | Population of city after 2 years. |
| 2. | How can we find out this? | First we find population after 1 year. |
| 3. | What is percentage increase in population every year? | 4% increase per year. |
| 4. | How can we find population at the end of first year. | Student can find that increase in population at the end of first year $= 50000 \times \frac{4}{100} = 2000$ |
| 5. | In this way what will be total population at the end of first Year? | Student tells answer 50000+2000 =52000 |
| 6. | Population increase for second year can be calculated on which figure? | Increase in population for second year can be calculated on 52000 |
| 7. | How can we calculate this increase? | Student can solve their efforts population increases at the end of second year $= 52{,}000 \times \frac{4}{100} = 2080$ |
| 8. | Now how to calculate the population at the end of second year? | Student will be able to understand that population of the two year will be =52000+2080 =54080 |

In this way solution to the given problem can be found by Heuristic method. Similarly other problem can also be solved?

**The place of Teacher in Heuristic Method**

In the opinion of student supporter of this method, the every student should be made a discoverer and inventor. According to them, it is a method of discovery. Therefore while using this method, the teacher should remain aside as an on looker and let the student select his own way to proceed onward. It means that teacher is a passive observe and student learns in his own manner. But it is extreme form of this method which is not very practical.

The student is after all a student. He is ignorant of many new things and cannot discover facts all alone by himself. He needs guidance and help of teacher at various steps. Therefore, it is not correct to say that here teacher should be passive observe. Actually without help and guidance of teacher the student cannot proceed properly at his own so teacher occupies an important place in this method though his role is confined to certain conditions as given below.

1. He is only to act as a guide.
2. He should not give the pupils the finished product of his own thinking.
3. He should carefully select the material and after his help in the form of question, suggestion and something direct telling.
4. The amount of help should be given just at necessary.
5. He should make a skillfully effort to develop heuristic attitude in student.
6. The teacher should have in mind the object of this method and help the child only when he has failed to overcome his difficulties by his own efforts.

**Procedure**

In this method there are not definite step to be followed some sort of the problem is given to student and a learning situation is created by the teacher. The students are told to solve the problem with their own efforts independently. By careful questioning the teacher may arouse the curiosity in the pupils and keep up their heuristic attitude.

## Merits of Heuristic Method

1 It involves active participation of student in the learning.

2 In this method student learns by doing, so the learnt concepts and cannot be forgotten.

3 It is based on the psychological fact that the student own experiences is the basis of real learning, so it is psychologically sound method.

4. In this method knowledge is not transmitted readymade but self- acquired, so it is assimilated, remembered and applied. Thus acquired knowledge is real and significant.

5. It inculcates in the student the interest for the subject and also develops willingness in them.

6. Discovering something by his own efforts and independent thinking student feel pride for his achievement.

7 It develops in students the heuristic and scientific attitude.

8 This method is based on the principle of activity.

## Demerits of Heuristic Method

1 It is not suitable for lower classes.

2 It is very slow method.

3 It is very lengthy method whole syllabus cannot be finished in time.

4. There is lack of text-book written on heuristic approach.

5 This is formational method rather than informational.

6. It needs extra-ordinary labour and special preparation from the teacher. Therefore every teacher may not be able to use it successfully.

## 2.1.5 Project Method

Project method is of American origin and it is an outcome of Dewey's philosophy of Pragmatism, However, this method is developed and applied practically by Dr. Kilpatrick.

The advocators of Project method believe that different branches of knowledge are different. Aspects of one whole and they are studied separately for the sake of convenience. More ever the exponents of the method contend that knowledge turns into power only through application.

### Definitions of Project

**Oxford Advanced Learners Dictionary-** Project is a plan of action; It usually involves a task of problem calling for constructive though or action or both.

**Dr. Kilpatrick-** A project is a whole-hearted purposeful activity proceeding in a social environment.

**J. A. Stevenson-** A project is a problematic act carried to completion in its natural setting.

All the definitions stated above emphasize that project should be a purposeful activity related to life & it should be carried out in a natural environment. In project method, teaching and learning is considered from the students point of view and in their natural setting. This method is an ideal way of promoting creativity, arousing and inculcating the spirit of equity among the student. However in this method teaching is more or less incidental.

### Basic Principle of Project Method

**1 Psychological principles of learning**

The project method is based on the Psychological Principles of learning namely.

(*i*) Learning by doing.

(*ii*) Learning by living.

(*iii*) Children learn better through association, cooperation & activity.

**Psychological Laws of learning**

The project method is based on the psychological laws of learning namely.

(*i*) Law of readiness.

(*ii*) Law of exercise.

(*iii*) Law of effect.

**Principal of activity**

Activity is a significant feature of this method. Children select, plan, execute & evaluate their. Project themselves.

**Principles of Social Experience**

The project should be selected from real life situations and every project should be social experience for the student.

**Principal of Reality**

The Project cannot be motivating and interesting for the learner unless it is natural and real from learners point of view.

**Principal of Utility**

Knowledge is meaning and worthwhile if it is practicable & useful.

**Steps of Project Method**

(*i*) Providing a situation.

(*ii*) Selecting and purposing of the Project.

(*iii*) Planning.

(*iv*) Executing.

(*v*) Evaluating.

(*vi*) Recording.

**Providing a situation**

The Project should arise out of the felt needs of the students. The teacher should provide such situations which may arouse some suitable questions to which the student seek answer. It should look important, must be interesting and purposeful for the student.

The Teacher can provide a vanity of situations through discussion, questioning library work field work etc.

**Selecting & Purposing**

The selection of the project is done by the students themselves. The teacher should refrain from purposing any project; otherwise the whole purpose of the method would be defected. However the teacher can guide the students in the selection of a good Project, keeping in mind the interest, aptitude and ability of the student. In this step the nature and goal of the project is clearing determined as well as the limits and scope of the project is clearly defined.

**Planning**

Planning involves the selection of the most appropriate set of activities to be executed. The student should choose the most practical plan of action. The student themselves should be the planning with the teacher as a guide.

While planning the points to be taken into consideration are

(*i*) The nature of and space of the project.

(*ii*) The degree of the complexity of the project.

(*iii*) Time allotted to finish the project

(*iv*) Availability of material recourses.

**Execution**

In this step the teacher help the student in assigning work to different students in accordance with their interest aptitude & capabilities. Each member of the group should be actively involved in the execution of the project. The teacher should carefully supervise and guide the student in the execution of the project as per the proposed plan action plan.

## Evaluation

The students alone with the teacher should review the progress of the project of the frequent intervals. This is to ensure that the student are progressing towards the realization of the objective of the projects without evaluation the project a move out of the focus.

## Recording

The students are required to maintain a complete record of work including the choice of the project; the planning, the discussion held and duties assigned. Also references books consulted and reading taken, difficulties faced, guidance sought, details of places visited and surveyed and so out should be carefully recorded.

## Criteria of good Project

A good project can be assessed using the following points.

1. The project should be purposeful, useful and practically applicable to the daily life of the students, with clear, well defined objectives.
2. The project should help in providing useful and meaningful in learning experience to each member of the group.
3. The project should be within the reach of the students in accordance with their interest and ability level.
4. The project should be feasible interest of availability of human and material resources and time limit.
5. The level of complexity of the project should match the ability level of the students.

## Role of Teacher

The teacher should assume the following rule while following Project method.

- Teacher guides students in selecting the project according to their interest aptitude and ability.
- Teacher helps students in planning and allotting activities to each member according to nature od abilities.

- Teacher helps to students when and where it is necessary.
- Teacher supervises and checks whether the project is running in time as planned.
- Teacher suggest extra resources if necessary for the successful execution of the project.
- Checks the record maintained by the students.

## Merits of Project Method

- It is based on sound psychological principles and laws of teaching.
- It provides scope for independent work and Individual development.
- It promotes habits of critical thinking and encourages the students to adopt problem solving method.
- It promotes social interaction inculcates sprit of cooperation and exchange of experiences among the students.
- It encourages practical applications of the subject, making the subject functional and meaningful to the learner.
- It provides opportunities for children to acquire a lot of skills observation, references, interpretation and so on.
- In this method children are active participants in learning task.

## Demerits of Project method

- Uneconomically in terms of time and it is not possible to fit in to the regular time table.
- Mathematics cannot be taught purely by this method. Incidental teaching will not suffice; planned teaching will have tube added to it.
- The student will not acquire skill and efficiency without collective and individual drill which will be possible through planned teaching only.
- There is no saving of time, energy and effort.
- Systematic and continuous teaching is not possible.

- It is likely to prove costly.
- Syllabus cannot be completed on time using this method.

**Some Project for Mathematics**

- Running co-operative bank in the school.
- Running stationery stores in the school.
- Planning for an annual camp.
- Laying a road.
- Planning and estimating the construction of a house.

## 2.1.6 Inductive - Deductive Method

### Inductive Method

Inductive method of teaching-learning mathematics is based on induction. In this method controversial truth is proved on the basics of particular to general rule. It is the method of constructing a formula with the help of sufficient number of concrete examples. Inductive method is more useful is version where principles, rules, definition, generalization and causal connections between facts are to be established.

This method is psychological in nature. The children follow the subject matter with great interest and understanding. In this method student himself attains the knowledge of helps of facts example and experiments. In this method we proceed from particular to general.

**Steps of Inductive Method**

**1. Presentation of Specific Examples**

In this steps teacher presents many examples of same type before the student and the solutions of those examples are obtained with the help of students. Students are asked to solve the examples with the help of unitary method.

**2. Observation**

After obtaining solutions of the various examples presented the students observe these and try to reach to some conclusion with the help of teacher.

### 3. Generalization

After observing the examples presented, the teacher and student decide some common formulae, principle, or law by logical mutual discussion

### 4. Testing and verification

After deciding some common formula or law, student verify the laws with the help of other examples or problems. In this way student logically attain the knowledge of inductive method by following above given steps.

**Example**

**Problem 1:-** Establishing a formula for solving simple interest problem.

### First step

Teacher will present many examples related to simple interest before students and will solve them by unitary method with the help of which the formula for simple interest can be established.

**Example 1 -** finds out S.I. of Rs. 700 at the rate of 8% per anum for 3 years.

**Solution**

1. What is S.I. of Rs. 100 for 1 year?

   - Rs.8

2. What will be S.I. of Rs. 1 for 1 Year?

$$\text{Rs.}\frac{8}{100}$$

3. What will be S.I. of Rs. 700 for 1 Year?

$$\text{Rs.}\frac{8}{100} \times 700$$

4. What will be S.I. of Rs. 700 for 3 Year?

$$\text{Rs.}\frac{8}{100} \times 700 \times 300$$

5. What will be the value?

$$\text{- Rs. } 8 \times 7 \times 3 = \text{Rs. } 168$$

**Example 1 -** finds out Simple Interest of Rs. 500 at the rate of 5% per anum for 4 years.

**Solution**

1. What is S.I. of Rs. 100 for 1 year?

   Rs.5

2. What will be S.I. of Rs. 1 for 1 Year?

$$\text{Rs.}\frac{5}{100}$$

3 What will be S.I. of Rs.500 for 1 Year?

$$\text{Rs.}\frac{5}{100}\times 100$$

4. What will be S.I. of Rs.500 for 4 Year?

$$\text{Rs.}\frac{5}{100}\times 100\times 4$$

5 What will be the value?

- Rs. 5 x 5 x 4 = Rs.100

Similarly, a number of examples of this type can be presented to the classroom.

**Second step**

Student will observe examples with the help of the Teacher.

**1 Teacher -**

What is S.I. for 3 year in example no.1?

**Student**

$$\text{S.I.} = \text{Rs.}\frac{8}{100}\times 700\times 3$$

$$= \text{Rs. } 168$$

**2 Teacher -**

What is S.I. for 4 year in example no.2?

**Student**

$$\text{S.I.} = \text{Rs.}\frac{5}{100}\times 500\times 4$$

Similarly by solving other more problems and by observing the process of finding out the interest, the students can arrive at a law or formula.

**Third step**

After observation of the given examples students will be able to establish the formula of simple interest.

For example. In example 1,

S.I. for 3 years $= \text{Rs.}\frac{8}{100} \times 700 \times 3$

In example 2, S.I. for 4 years

$$= \text{Rs.}\frac{5}{100} \times 500 \times 4$$

**Now the teacher can make following discussion :-**

**Q. 1** What is 8 and 5 in the given examples?

**Ans** 8 and 5 are the rate of interest.

**Q. 2** What is 700 and 500 in the given examples?

**Ans.** 700 and 500 are the principal.

**Q. 3** What is 3 and 4 in the given examples?

**Ans.** 3 and 4 are the years or time.

Therefore we can write;

$$\text{S.I.} = \frac{\text{Rate x Principal x Time}}{100}$$

$$\text{S.I.} = \frac{\text{Rate x Principal x Time}}{100}$$

OR,

We can write,

$$\text{S.I.} = \frac{\text{Rate x Principal x Time}}{100}$$

OR

$$\text{S.I} = \frac{\text{PX N x T}}{100}$$

**Fourth step**

Student will be able to verify the derived formula by solving other problem of simple interest based on this formula.

**For example -** find out S.I. of Rs.1500 at the rate of 9% per yearly for 18 years.

**Solution (1) —Using the formula**

Simple Interest $= \frac{P \times R \times T}{100}$

$= \frac{1500 \times 9 \times 18}{100}$

= Rs. 15x9x18

= Rs.2430

**Solution (2)**

PRT = Rs. (1500) x (9 % Per years) x (18 Year) 9

= Rs.1500 x " $\frac{9}{100}$ Per Year x 18 Year

= Rs. 15 x 9 x 18

= Rs. 2430

In this way students will be able to determine and verify the formula of simple interest with the help of different examples. Similarly with the help of different examples the formula for compound interest and other formula can be determined and generalized in the classroom.

**Example 2 :-**

Teacher will teach rule relating to indices of multiplication when the base is same by inductive method as below:-

**Step 1-** (Presentation of specific examples)

Teacher will present examples of multiplication of index numbers whose base are same and will write the solutions of examples on blackboard by taking students active and verbal participation

Teacher:- Write $3^4$ in multiplication form?

Student :- 3 x 3 x 3 x 3 x 3

Teacher :- Now write $3^3$ in multiplication form?

Student :- 3 x 3 x 3

Teacher :- Write $3^4$ x $3^3$in multiplication form?

Student :- 3 x 3 x 3 x 3 x 3 x 3 x 3

Teacher :- How many times multiplication of 3 is in above examples ?

**Student :- 7 -**

**Teacher :-** How you will write multiplication of 3 for 7 times in Index form?

**Student :- $3^7$**

In the same Teacher will solve following examples with the help of student and plot a table as following

| Ex.No. | Example | Multiplication form | Solution |
|---|---|---|---|
| 1 | $3^4$ x $3^3$ | 3 x 3 x 3 x 3 x 3 x 3 x 3 | $3^7$ |
| 2 | $2^2$ x $2^3$ | 2 x 2 x 2 x 2 x 2 | $2^5$ |
| 3 | $(\frac{2}{5})^5$x $(\frac{2}{5})$ | $\frac{2}{5}$ x $\frac{2}{5}$x $\frac{2}{5}$ x $\frac{2}{5}$ x $\frac{2}{5}$ x $\frac{2}{5}$ | $(\frac{2}{5})^6$ |
| 4 | $a^3$ x $a^3$ | a x a x a x a x a x a | $a^6$ |

**Step 2 - (Observation)**

Student will observe examples and solutions written in the table.

Teacher will ask following question

**Teacher -**What you will say about the base of example problem and solution?

**Student -** base of both is same

**Teacher -** What you will say about the Index of example problem and solution?

**Student -**Index of Index number of solution is addition of index of index number of example problem.

While giving these answers students will do comparative observation and brain storming.

**Step 3- (Generalization)**

After observation and brain storming of the given examples student will be able to establish rule of indices for multiplication when the base is same.

For motivation of generalization teacher takes following example

**Teacher -** write $a^m$ x $a^n$ in multiplication form?

**Student** — a x a x a x a..... .....(m times) x a x a x a xa......... (n times)

**Teacher** — How you will write this in Index form?

**Student** — $a^m \times a^n = a^{m+n}$

**(Teacher concludes)** — Thus we see that multiplying numbers having the same base, the base of product remains the same and the indices are added to get the index of the product.

Student prepares rule of Indices for multiplication when the base is same is as follows

If a is any rational number and 'm' and 'n' are any positive integers then,

$a^m \times a^n = a^{m+n}$

**Step 4 - (Testing and Verification)**

Students will be able to verify the derived formula by solving other examples of multiplication of index numbers when the base is same.

$(2/5)^7 \times (2/3)^8 = (2/7)^{7+8} = (2/7)^{15}$

$a^{10} \times a^7 = a^{10+7} = a^{17}$

In this way student will be able to determine and verify the formula for of Indices for multiplication when the base is same with of different examples.

**Merits of Inductive Method**

- Inductive method helps to generalize formulae and rule on the basic of a concrete examples.
- It is most useful for beginners.
- It is based on psychological and logical thinking.
- It improves student's observation and generalization skill.
- Due to this method students remain active during teaching-learning process.
- Due to this method no need of cramming formula, principle. If forget formulae he can prepare formula with certain examples.

- Due to this method correlation between Students-Student, Student-Teacher increases.
- It helps in clarifying any doubt about the 'how & why' of formula in the very beginning.

**Demerits of Inductive Method**

- Induction does not prove but only provides the material to prove; it discovers.
- This method is more time consuming & it needs much labour.
- Its application is limited to very few topics in mathematics where actual observation of the particular instances is possible.
- This method is not suitable for higher order mathematics principles cannot be generalized through the observation of concrete cases.
- This method is not useful for advanced level of teaching.

**Deductive Method**

Deductive method is exactly opposite of inductive method. Deductive logic is used in this method. This method is based on deductive reasoning. Deductive reasoning is the process of drawing logical inferences from established facts or fundamental assumptions. Deductive method is mainly used in algebra, Geometry and trigonometry because different relations, laws and formulae are used in these sub-branches of mathematics. It is impossible to verify each law and formula practically. In this method help is taken from assumptions, postulates and axioms of mathematics.

**Procedure -** In deductive method we proceed from 'abstract to concrete' from general to particular' and from 'general rule to example'.In this method,principle,law, formulae and relations are presented before the student in real form. Student learns the told law, principle and formulae by heart.

**Steps of Deductive Method**

Deductive method of teaching follows the steps given bellow:-

(*a*) Presentation of rule or formula - The teacher writes the formula on black board then gives problem relating to formula.

(*b*) Application - the Teacher solves few problems with the help of the formula on the blackboard by which student can learn how to use the formula.

(*c*) Inference - After getting proper solution of the problems with the help of given formula the student came to understand that this formula is the key to solve this type of formula.

Generally teacher gives the knowledge of the facts to the students such as

Formula for simple interest is -

$$S.I. = \frac{\text{Rate x Principal x Time}}{100}$$

**Example -1:** find out the interest on Rs. 500 at the rate of 5% for 2 years.

**Solution** — In deductive method students are told the formula of calculation of S. I. so the student find the solution suitably and in less time.

According to this method the given example can be solved by proceeding as follows.

Formula for simple interest is -

$$S.I. = \frac{\text{Rate x Principal x Time}}{100}$$

In the given example

Principle = Rs. 500, Rate = 5% and Time= 2 years

$$\text{Simple interest is - } S.I. = \frac{500 \times 5 \times 2}{100}$$

$$= \text{Rs. } 5x5x2$$

$$= \text{Rs. } 50$$

**Example No. 2**

Teacher will present the formula of law of indices of multiplication

$a^m \text{ x } a^n = a^{m+n}$

Solve the following example

(*i*) $\left(\frac{1}{4}\right)^4 \times \left(\frac{1}{4}\right)^2$

(*ii*) $7^3$ X $7^2$

**Merits**

1. This method is simple for the students as they get a readymade key to solve the relevant problems.
2. It save time and labour for both the teacher and the students.
3. It enhances speed skill and efficiency in solving problems.
4. It is short and elegant method.
5. It helps in fixation of formula and rules as it provide adequate opportunities for practice and revision.
6. It completes the induction is reduced to certainty in deduction.
7. It is useful for higher classes.

**Demerits**

1. It encourages a rote memory as deductive method demands the use of certain laws rules or formula to be recalled by the learners from their memory.
2. It does not clarify the doubts of the students regarding the generalization and hence learning remains incomplete.
3. It is not suitable for beginners.
4. It does not encourage student's involvement in learning.
5. It is not suitable for the development for thinking, reasoning and discovery.

### 2.1.7 Analytic and Synthetic Method

The word 'analytic' is derived from the word 'analysis' which means 'breaking up' or resolving a thing into its constituent elements. Analysis starts with "what we have to find out and traces the connection between it and the data. With the help of this method the difficult parts of any problem can be analyzed to find out the solution of the given problem. Thus separation of different parts of a problem is known as analysis. In this method we processed form 'unknown to known' or form 'conclusion to hypothesis' in this way we reach to the conclusion. This method is used in the following conditions.

- When we have to prove any theorem.
- When construction work is to be done in the geometry.
- When we have to find out the solution of some new arithmetical problems.

In this method every step has its own importance and reason therefore analysis of problem should be done properly. Thus in this method first of all one has to know 'what is to be found out?' obviously it is unknown for the learners. Then we think of further steps or possibilities that may connect the unknown with the known thus we seek the requirements to get the values of unknown. In this process one requirement leads to other requirements and thus we reach to the ultimate requirement which is known or given in the question. Therefore it is the process of unfolding of the problem to known its hidden aspects.

Application of Analytic method in mathematics

**Example no.: 1**

To prove that the diagonals of a parallelogram bisect each other.

**Analysis**

First of all we will draw a parallelogram ABCD and its diagonals AC and BD which intersects each other at a point O.

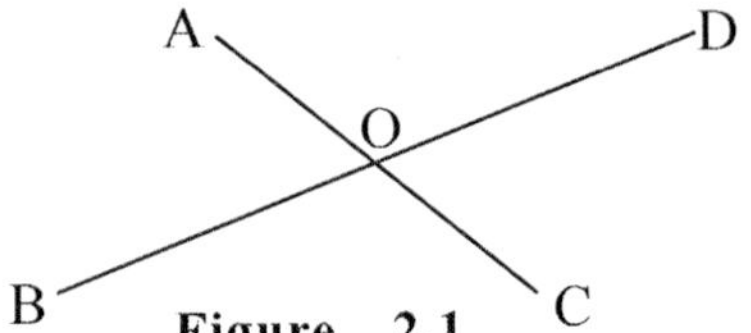


**Figure 2.1**

**Now we will proceed with question and answer as follow**

| | | |
|---|---|---|
| (i) | What is given? | A parallelogram ABCD whose diagonals AC & BD intersect each other at point 0 |
| (ii) | What is to be proved? | It is to be proved that the diagonal AC & BD bisects each other. |
| (iii) | How can it be proved? | BD bisect each other. If we prove OA = OC & OD = OB |
| (iv) | How can it be proved | By proving the congruency of triangle which have side OA, OC & OD, OB |
| (v) | Which are triangle in the diagram have side OA, OC OD, & OB | Diagonal AC & BD intersects each other at point o and thus two triangles viz OAB & OCD are formed having the sides OA, OB & OC, OD respectively. Therefore if the triangles OAB & OCD can be proved as congruent then OA & OC will be equal and similarly OB & OD will be equal as these are the corresponding sides of two congruent triangle. |

Therefore we have to prove the OAB & OCD are congruent

In the OAB & OCD

$\angle AOB = \angle COD$ (opposite angles)

$\angle OAB = \angle OCD$

(AB || CD hence these are corresponding angle)

AB = CD (opposite side of Parallelogram)

Thus A OAB ≅ A OCD

Therefore OA = OC & OB = OD

Thus it is proved that diagonals of a parallelogram bisect each other.

**Example no.: 2**

If $\frac{a}{b} = \frac{c}{d}$

Then prove

$$\frac{ac + 4b^2}{bc} = \frac{c^2 + 4bd}{dc}$$

**Analysis**

We have to start from equation that is to be proved and proceed towards the known. Thus we start from

$$\frac{ac + 4b^2}{bc} = \frac{c^2 + 4bd}{dc}$$

1. How to write this identity in easy from? (We cut 'c' in the denominators of both sides and then cross multiply)

Thus $\frac{ac + 4b^2}{bc} = \frac{c^2 + 4bd}{dc}$

or $\frac{ac + 4b^2}{b} = \frac{c^2 + 4bd}{d}$

by cross multiplying

$acd + 4b^2 d = c^2b + 4b^2d$

2 How can it be solved further?

($4^2bd$ can be cancelled from both side and 'c' can also be Cut).

$acd + 4b^2d = c^2b + 4b^2d$

$\therefore$ $acd = c^2b$

$\therefore$ $ad = bc$

3. How can we write it in some other form?

$ad = cb$

OR $\frac{a}{b} = \frac{c}{d}$

(This type of solution of the problems can be easily obtained by analysis)

**3 Example of analytic method In Arithmetic**

**Example no.: 3**

If length and breadth of a field are 50m and 20m respectively. There is a 5m wide path enclosing the field find out the area of the path.

***Answer: Solution by Analytic Method***

**ANSWER - SOLUTION BY ANALYTIC METHOD -**

1. What is given in the question?

   → (Length and Breadth of a rectangular field and width of the path)

**2.** What is length of the field ? length of the field = 50m

**3.** What is breadth of the field ?
Breadth of the field = 20m

**4.** What is Width of the path ? = 5m.
Width of the path = 5m.
We can draw a diagram according to given thing?

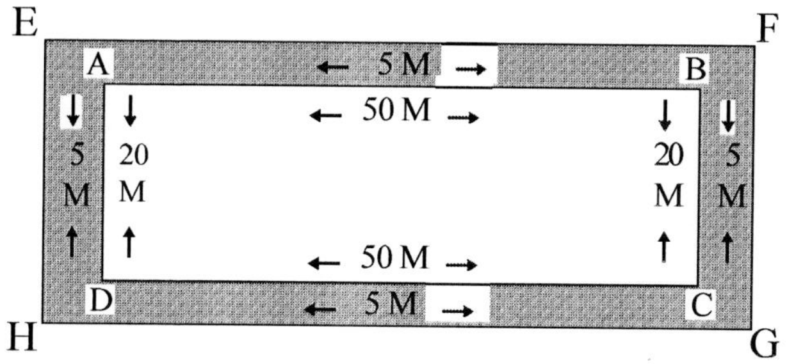


**Figure 2.2**

**5.** What has to be calculated in the given question?
→ Area of the shaded porition.

**6.** How we can find the area of Path enclosing the field?
→ If area of the field • ABCD is subtracted from the area of the field EFGH with the area of Path.

**7.** How do we find out the area of field including path?
→ If length & breath of paths are known.

**8.** How do we find out the length and breadth of the path?
→ By adding twice of the width of Path in length and breadth of the field.

**9.** What will be length & breadth of field EFGH.?
→ (length = 50 + 5 + 5 = 60m
Breadth = 20 + 5 + 5 = 30m)

**10.** What will be area of field EFGH?
→ Area of field EFGH = L x B
= 60m x 30m = 1800m$^2$

**11.** What will be area of field ABCD?

→ Area of field ABCD = L x B = 50m x 20m = $1000m^2$

**12.** What will be area of Path or shaided area?

→ Area of Path or of shaided area

Area of field EFGH – Area of field ABCD

= 1800 – 1000

= $800m^2$

***Merits and Demerits of Analytic Method: Merits***

- This method is based on psychological Principal.
- This method helps in developing reasoning and decision making power of the learner.
- It facilitates understanding as the learner has to go through the whole process themselves.
- It is a discovery method since here learner has to work as a discoverer of the facts.
- In this method learner is more active and thus his participation is encouraged automatically.
- It leaves no doubts and convinces the learner.
- Here each step has its reason and justification and therefore no cramming is required.
- By this method, the teacher can carry whole class with him.
- In this method learner throughout faces with the question like, 'How can it be proved?', 'How can it be done?', 'What are the possible way for it?', 'How can it be resolved into simpler elements?' etc. Thus it helps the learner to tackle the problem confidently and intelligently.
- In this method there is very little scope of forgetting.

***Demerits***

- It is lengthy and time consuming.
- Here facts are not presented in any set pattern. Thus, there is a lack of systematization.

- With this method, acquirement of speed of and efficiency is difficult.
- This method isn't suitable for each & every topic of mathematics.
- This method is not fruitful for below average students.
- Every teacher cannot use this method successfully.

***Synthetic Method***

The word synthetic is derived from the word 'Synthesis' which means to combine to gather. Thus in meaning, synthetic is opposite of analytic. But in practice, it is the complement of analytic. In synthetic method, we proceed from know to unknown. Synthesis is a process of placing things together that area a part. So here we combine together a number of facts, perform certain mathematical operations and then arrive at the desired result or solution of the problem. In this method one has to start with something already known and connect that with the unknown part of the statement. Thus it is the process of putting together known bits of information to reach the point where unknown information become obvious and true. Therefore, here we start with the data, available and connect it with the conclusion.

**Example :-** (as a comparative study earlier examples given for analytic method are presented here again)

To prove that the diagonals of a parallelogram bisect each other.

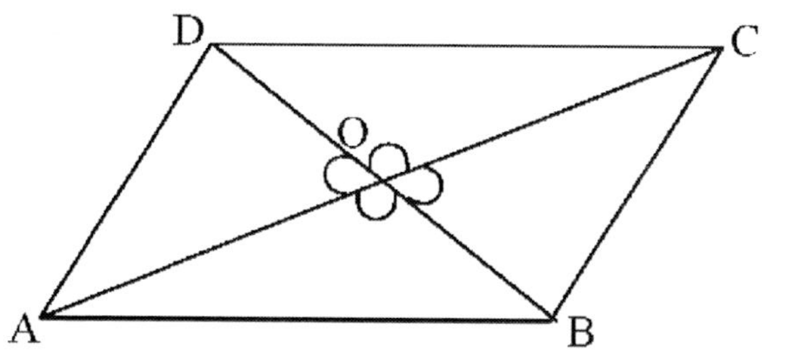


**Figure 2.3**

Given :- A parallelogram ABCD whose diagonals AC and BC Intersects each other at a point O

To prove → AO = OC and BO = OD

Prove:- In the triangle AOB and COD

AOB = COD (vertically opposite angles)

OAB = OCD (corresponding angles)

AB = CD (opposite sides of a parallelogram)

Hence $\Delta OAB \cong \Delta\ OCD$

ThereforeAO = OC & BO = OD prove

**Example: 2**

If $\frac{a}{b} = \frac{c}{d}$ then prove

$$\frac{ac + 4b^2}{bc} = \frac{c^2 + 4bd}{dc}$$

**Solution:-**

We know that $\frac{a}{b} = \frac{c}{d}$ thus in this method we start from known and proceed to unknown.

Adding $\frac{4b}{c}$ on both side c

$$\frac{a}{b} + \frac{4b}{c} = \frac{c}{d} + \frac{4b}{c}$$

ac + 4b d + c

$$ac + \frac{4b^2}{bc} = \frac{c^2 4bd}{cd}$$ is proved

**Note**

No logic or reason is gives here for why $\frac{4b}{c}$ is added on both side

**Example: 3**

Length and breadth of a field is 50m and 20m respectively. A path enclosing the field has a width of 5m find out the area of path.

**Solution**

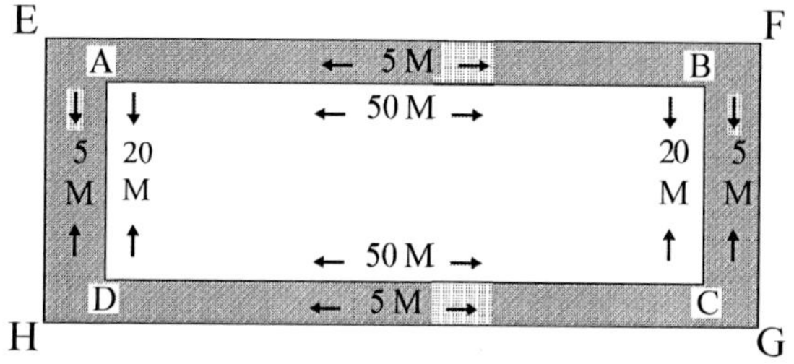


**Figure 2.4**

**Given:**

Length of field = 50m

Breadth of field = 20m

Width of path = 5m

To find Areas of path ?

Proof

Length of field with path = (5 + 50 + 5) m

= 60m

Breadth of field with path = (5 + 20 + 5) m

= 30m

Area of field including path = 60 x 30

= $1800m^2$

Area of field = 50 x 20

= $1000m^2$

Area of path = Area of Including path – Area of field

= $1800m^2 - 1000m^2$

= $800m^2$

Here no logic or Explanation is given for why length and breadth of field will be 60m & 30m respectively and why area & path will be $800m^2$.

***Merits of Synthetic Method***

**Merits**

- It is short and quick method.
- It glorifies the memory of the field.

- It formulates record and presents concisely the discovered facts.
- This is the method of setting out the solution in concise form.
- It is informative method.
- It takes less time.

**Demerits**

- In this method, there is no scope of discovery.
- It leads to Rote memory.
- It creates many doubts in the mind of the student.
- It does not give full satisfaction to the student.
- There are no opportunities for developing thinking reasoning and other mental abilities.
- The recall of each step cannot be possible for every child.

***# Comparision of Analytic & Synthetic Method #***

| No. | Analytic | Synthetic |
|---|---|---|
| 1 | Analysis means breaking up into components | Synthetic means combining the elements to get something new. |
| 2 | Leads from unknown to known | Leads from known to unknown. |
| 3 | A method of discovery and thought. | A method for the presentation of discovered facts. |
| 4 | Lengthy, laborious and time consuming | Short, concise and elegant. |
| 5 | Valid reasons to justify every step in the sequence. | No justification for every step in the sequence. |
| 6 | Encourages meaningful learning. | Encourages role learning. |
| 7 | Easy to re discover. | Once forgotten, not easy to recall |

| | | |
|---|---|---|
| 8 | Encourages originality of thinking and reasoning. | Encourages memory work. |
| 9 | A psychological method. | A logical method. |
| 10 | Application of inductive reasoning | Application of deductive reasoning |
| 11 | Process of thinking | Product of thinking. |

### 2.1.8 Question Method

Question method is known as Socrates method there is one meaningful statement about Socrates is that. 'He taught everything but told nothing situation. Questioning is also an important teaching skill. An effective teacher employs questioning technique appropriately and also prepares good question.

In mathematics each concept can be explained with student's related daily life. Even by asking proper question on preknowledge teacher can takes to students towards new teaching units. By using this method teacher can keep students active by both ways. (Verbal and active Response) so it is very important and useful in mathematics teachings. For effective using to this method teacher should have knowledge of types of questions, defective forms of questions and ways of asking question.

*Types of Question*

**1. Introductory Question**

These questions are used in Introducing new topic or lesson to his student. The Introducing questions are based on previous knowledge which is related to new knowledge. These employ from known to unknown maximum of teaching.

**2. Developing Question**

After introducing new topics some question are asked to develop the new content. It employs from logical to psychological techniques of teaching.

### 3. Recapitulatory Question

Those question are called recapitulatory questions by which the main factual points of the lesson are revised. The aim of these questions is to substaniate the knowledge by organizing it properly. From this point of view, these questions should be based on the taught knowledge.

### 4. Evaluatory Question

At the end of lesson the teacher asks questions to the test of knowledge of the learners to assimilate deather they could learn the content generally oral question are asked.

### *Characterstics of Good Question*

An effective should be able to construct and to use good question. Preparation of good question requires insight, experience, metal activity and awareness of teaching problem. A teacher should have the full understanding of good questions. The following are the main characteristics of good question.

(*i*) The language of question should be simple and understandable.

(*ii*) The form of question should be straight forward.

(*iii*) The question should have the definite meaning.

(*iv*) The question should be arranged in logical sequence. It should be psychological workable.

(*v*) The question should serve the purpose of teaching learning.

(*vi*) The question should have the utility from learners and content point of view.

### *Some Defectives forms of Question*

The question plays an important role in organizing teaching activities. The defective question makes presentation ineffective or do not serve purpose of teaching some defectives forms of question are following.

### 1. Echo Question

An Echo questions is a type of direct question that repeats part or all of something which someone else has just said. Also called a parrot question. for example. Is the capital of India New Delhi? It is very simple to answer such question. These questions do not serve any purpose of teaching. A teacher should not use such question in his classroom presentation.

**2. Yes or no type question**

This from of question requires answer inYes or No. for example, Is the sum of three angles of triangle is 180?

Is this poem having national feelings? The answer of such question is based on unthinking mental process.

**3. Rhetorical Question**

This form of question uses flowery language. Generally inexperience teacher make use of such defective question in his presentation. for example. President of country committed to serve the nation as the first citizen.

Such question does not provide the situation to learn for though providing ideas.

**4. Indefinite Question**

This form of question does not known the definite answer. Such question creates confusion in the mind of learners. Such type of defective question has the adverse effect on the minds of learners.

There may be several type of defective questions which do not serve type of defective questions which do not serve the purpose of teaching.

### *Way of Asking Question*

The ways of asking question is an art. It is a teacher skill. Experienced and Intellegent teacher can ask questions in learning teaching Process skillfully to make teaching effective. Every teacher should kept following things in mind while asking question in classroom presentation.

1. The question should be asked in general addressing to the whole class. It should not be addressed by name a student. The purpose

of asking a question is to make attentive each and every student of the class.

2. There should be evenly distribution of question over the class. Each students of class should feel that he may be asked question. Therefore he remain active in the presentation of teacher in the class.
3. In asking question and recurring the answer appropriate time should be given. A teacher should not make hurry in this can text.
4. A teacher should not repeat his questions. he should ask once in the class.
5. A teacher should not use unnecessary words before asking question e.g. yes, what you feel? or who can answer this question.

Question method is used in each method of mathematics teaching but some topic are such; that they can taüght very effectively by question method like rules of Indices, Derivation of formulae, types of set, Concepts of Indices, Polynomial, formula of Area of triangle quadrilateral circle and on theorems of triangle and circle.

## 2.2 MODELS OF TEACHING

Gage (1987) defined, " teaching as an interpersonal influence aimed at changing the ways on which other person can or will behave" Though this definition stresses the involvement of more than one person in the teaching process and the behavioral influence of one person in changing the behavior of others, it does not specify the person involved in teaching. A Similar view is given by Hough and Duncan (1970) in their definition with a difference, when they define teaching as "an activity, in which one creatively and imaginatively uses himself and his knowledge to promote the learning and welfare of others "in this definition the authors have stressed the involvement of more than one person in the teaching act, and given teaching the status of a professional, rational activity.

Flanders (1970) says "the act of teaching leads to reciprocal contacts between the teacher and the pupils and the involved in the teaching; it does not specify the situation in which the teaching takes place and the kind of activities performed in teaching. These aspects are affected in the definition given by Cater V, Good in the Dictionary of Education. Good has given narrow and broader meanings of teaching. According to the narrow meaning, teaching refers to the act of instructing in educational institutions. Under the broader meaning teaching implies the management by an instructor of the teaching-learning process including. A) Direct interaction between teacher and learner. B) The proactive decision making process of planning designing, and preparing the materials for the teaching-learning conditions and. C) post-active redirection (evaluation, redesign and dissemination). From Good's definition three major factors emerges.

Teaching is an instructional activity that takes place in an educational institution.

It is a managerial activity which is concerned with organization of teaching-learning situations.

It is an interactive process between the teacher and the student which involves preactive decision making activities and post-active redirections.

## Teaching as a process

Teaching as process has been highlighted by Joyce and Well when they defined teaching "as a process by which the teacher and students create a shared environment including sets of values, beliefs (agreement about what is improvement) which in turn colour their view of reality. "This definition, adds a new dimension to teaching namely the importance of teaching-learning environment. But teaching as a process is not clear from the definition. But a study of the four phases of teaching given by Hough ans Duncan makes it clear that teaching is process which has a series of activities that take place logically and sequentially as given in tables.

**Table 1. Phases of Teaching (Hough and Duncan)**

| Curriculum Planning Phase Phase-I | Instructing Phase Phase-II | Measuring Phase Phase-III | Evaluating Phase Phase-IV |
|---|---|---|---|
| Helping to formulate goals of education | Creating intention regarding the strategies of instruction | Creating or selecting devices to measure student learning. | Using feedback to evaluation appropriation of objectives |
| Selecting & organization the contact of instruction | Instruction | Measuring student learning. | Effectiveness of instruction. |
| Stating the objects of instruction | Obtaining situational feedback about instructing. | Organising & analyzing data. | The validity and reliability of measurement. |

Thus Hough and Duncan in the four phases of teaching make it clear that teaching is a process of a series of activities which take place in a logical sequence.

## Components of Teaching

The three components involved in the teaching act are the teacher, the student & the curriculum. All components of teaching play an equally import role in the process of teaching-learning.

## Emergence of Models of Teaching

Attempts have been made by researchers to match the different approaches or strategies or styles of learning with the objectives of instruction & learning styles. Competence in teaching stems from the capacity to reach out to differing children & to create a rich & multidimensional environment for them. Models of teaching emerged out of the search by Joyce & Well find a variety of approach or strategies to match the various learning styles.

### 2.2.1 Concept of Models of Teaching :

The world 'model' is used by people in different ways in different contexts. In the teaching-learning process, models have the same interpretation as they have in case of construction of dams, buildings etc. Thus models of teaching like plans, patterns or blueprints present the steps necessary to bring about a desired outcome. According to Joyce & Well, a teaching mode is a pattern or plan which can be used to shape curriculum or course, to design instructional materials and to guide a teacher's actions. A part from the above uses it creates the necessary environment which facilitates the teaching process. The core of the process of teaching is the arrangement of environment within which the students can interact. Thus a model of teaching consists of guidelines for designing educational activities & environments. In specific of teaching & learning that are intended to achieve certain kinds of goals. Thus a model of teaching is designed to achieve a particular set of objectives and not a substitute to any teaching skill.

## Characteristics of Teaching Models

### *Models of teaching*

Are some sort plans or guidelines or patterns or strategies of teaching?

Are Systematic procedures to modify the behavior of the learners?

Specify the learning outcomes in terms of observable & measurable performance of students.

Specify in define terms the environmental conditions under which a student's response should be observed.

Specify the criteria of acceptable performance expected from the students.

### *Families of Models*

Joyce and Well classified models of teaching into four families that represent distinct orientations towards people and how they learn. They are

Information Processing Models

Personal Models

Social Interaction Models &

Behavioral models.

### *Concept Attainment Model*

The content a teacher transacts in a classroom can be broadly classified into three categories, namely facts, concepts and generalizations. Though the process of acquiring these three types of content by the pupils is not uniform, mostly teachers use the same strategy for teaching these three types of content.

Helping children learn concepts efficiently is a fundamental purpose of education. Until recently, however, most educators did not consciously distinguish the learning of concepts from other types of learning. However Bruner and his associates have done substantial work in determining the process of learning concepts and indentified the process. Based on the work or Bruner and his associates, Joyce and Well (1980) developed a model which is known as the Concept Attainment Modle.

### *Concepts, Facts and Generalizations Differentiated*

Concept of a thing is what it means to an individual or a mental image of the thing formed by a generalization from particulars. De Cecco (1980) defined concept as a class of stimuli which have common characteristics.

Triangles, prime numbers, glass, plate, chalk, tree etc., are all concepts. Bruner and his associates asserted that we encounter innumerable stimuli in our environment and we respond to them in terms of their class membership rather than their uniqueness. In other words we from categories of objects or events on the basis of their common characteristics and these categories are known as concepts.

Facts are singular occurrences which either occurred in the past or exist in the present and which have no predictive validity. For example, statements such as "India got independence in 1947", "Tamil Nadu is one of the states of India" are all facts.

A generalization is an inferential statement which expresses a relationship of two or more concepts, applies to more than one event and has a predictive and explanatory value. For instance the statement "when a transversal cuts two parallel lines, the alternate angles are equal" is a generalization.

***Theory of concepts***

Burner and his associates assumed that though the concept of categories may differ from culture, the thought process of forming categories will be the same. Therefore, they assumed that the process of acquiring concept is essentially the same in all cultures. Similarly the thoughts process of forming concept is the same for individuals in different cultures.

According to Burner, a concept has the following five elements:-

Name of the concept
Examples (Positive and Negative)
Attributes (Essential and Non-essential)
Attribute Value
Rules

Understanding a concept means knowing all the elements of the concept. The name is the term given to a category or concept. For example, the category of rectilinear figures bounded by four line segments is called as 'quadrilateral' and hence the term quadrilateral refers to the concept/category. Items which are grouped in a single category may differ from one another in certain aspects. But they will have certain common features and it is because of these common features that they are given the one general name.

Example refers to the instance of the concept. Instances may be positive or negative. Positive instances demonstrate what the concept is, whereas negative instances demonstrate what the concept is not. Attaining the concept requires the individual to classify the instances as instances ***and non-instances as non-instances of the concept.***

The third and fourth elements of a concept are attributes and attributes values. Attributes refer to characteristic features of a concept. An attributes any discrete feature of an event and can be used as a means of inferring the identify of something. Attribute of concepts may have a range of values. For example, the attribute of 'quadrilateral' may be represented by the values square, rectangle, parallelogram, etc. However, there are concepts whose attribute do not have a range of values.

The fifth element of a concept is the rule. A rule is a definition or statement specifying the essential attributes of concepts. For instance 'Polygon' is a concept. The definition of polygon is the rule. A rule normally evolves at the end of the concept attainment process.

***Concept Attainment Teaching***

In concept attainment teaching situation the learner is presented with an array of instance or examples that are a like in some ways, and different in others. The learner encounter these examples and must find out or be told whether each instance **simplifies** the concept. At each encounter with an instance, the learner **formulate** and reformulates a hypothesis about the concept. Each instance or example provides potential information about the character and attribute values of the concept. The process of sorting Yes and No instance is the core of the Concept of the model is to help the students attain concepts, a second purpose of the concept attainment model is to acquaint student with the conceptualizing process itself.

In indentifying the thinking strategies people attain concepts, Bruner and his associates distinguished between the two learning conditions of selection and reception. In selection condition, the examples are not marked 'yes or no'. The learner encountering the array of unmarked examples selects one and inquires whether it is a 'yes' or a 'no'. In reception conditions, the teacher presents the examples in a pre arranged order labeling them 'yes or no'.

Science people use different strategies to attain; Concept Attainment Model has three variations.

Reception Model
Selection Model
Unorganized Material Model
Reception Model

In the Reception Model of teaching, the teacher presents an array of examples/ instance (positive) and non-examples/ non instances (negative). The examples are labeled as 'Yes' and the non-examples as 'No' and are presented one by one. At each encounter, the learners compare attributes in positive and negative instance and formulate and reformulate hypotheses with regard to the concept. They are asked by the teacher to name the concept and state the rule / definition of the concept according to its essential attributes. The teachers can extant support to the students in case students find any difficulty in naming the concept or stating the rule.

After this the teacher parents an array of unlabelled examples, requiring the learners to label them as 'Yes' or 'No'. To ensure complete learning thereafter, the students are asked to give a few examples of the concept on their own. The teacher then asks the students to analysis the strategies that they have followed to attain the concept. Students may be asked to compare the effectiveness of different strategies.

***Syntax of Reception Model***

The phases and activities of the Reception Model concept attainment are outlined in table. 8T2. The activities involved in the Reception Model can be divided into the phases.

In the first phase the teacher present labeled example (Yes) and non- examples (No) of the concept to be formed. Students are asked to compare the attributes in positive and negative examples and identify the attributes which are present in all the positive examples. They are asked to formulate and test hypotheses about the concept. Finally the learners are asked to name the concept and state the rule defining the concept.

In phase two, students test their attainment of the concept first by correctly identifying additional unlabelled examples of the concept and then by generating their own examples.

In phase three, the students are asked to analyze the strategies by which they attain concepts.

**Table Syntax of the Reception Model**

| Phase I | Phase II | Phase III |
|---|---|---|
| Presentation of Data & Identification of concept | Testing Attainment of the concept | Analysis of Thinking Strategies |
| Teacher presents labeled examples | Students identify additional examples as 'yes' or 'no' | Student describe thoughts |
| Students compare attributes in positive & negative example | Teacher confirms hypotheses, names concept, & restates definition according to essential attributes | Students discuss the role of hypotheses & attributes |
| Students generate & test hypotheses | Students generate examples | Student discuss type & number of hypotheses |
| Student state a definition according to the essential attributes | | |

### *Social System of the Model*

The model has a moderate structure. When using the Reception Model of Concept Attainment the teacher acts as a recorder, keeping track of the hypotheses (concept) as they are mentioned and of the attributes. The teacher also supplies additional examples as needed. The three major functions of the teacher during reception-oriented concept attainment activity are to record, prompt (cue), and present additional data.

### *Principles of Reaction*

During the flow of the lesson, the teacher wants to be supportive but emphasizes hypothetical nature of discussion. The teacher helps to create a dialogue in which students test their hypotheses against each other. In the latter phases of the model, the teacher wishes to turn the student's attention towards analysis of specific features of examples. The teacher assists the students in discussing and their thinking strategies again begin very supportive.

### *Support System*

Support system consists of material that has been designed so that concepts are embedded in the material, with positive and negative examples that can be pointed out to the student. In this model, students do not invent new concepts, but attain the ones that have previously been selected by the teacher. Hence the data source need to be known before hand and the aspects of concept attainment activity made visible.

### *The Selection-Oriented Model*

In the selection-oriented model the teacher presents an array of examples. Unlike in the Reception Model these examples are not labeled as 'yes' or 'no'. A learner conformed with the examples, selects one and enquires whether it is an 'yes' or 'no'. The major difference between Reception Oriented and Selection Oriented models is in the labeling and sequencing of examples. Another difference is that in Selection Oriented Models students may ask about their own examples in order to attain the concept. The students also control the sequence of the examples by choosing the ones they want to inquire about. The Selections Models place responsibility for concept attainment and attribute tracking in the hands of the students. Its syntax is similar to that of Reception Model, but its activities and roles within phases one and two are slightly different as shown in table 3.

**Table Syntax of the Selection Model Concept Attainment**

| Phase I | Phase II | Phase III |
|---|---|---|
| Presentation of Data & Identification of attributes | Testing Attainment of the concept | Analysis of Thinking Strategies |
| Teacher presents unlabeled examples | Students identify unlabeled examples | Student describe thoughts |

| Phase I | Phase II | Phase III |
|---|---|---|
| Students enquires which examples including their own, are positive | Students generate examples | Students discuss the role of hypotheses & attributes |
| Students generate & test hypotheses | Teacher confirms hypotheses, names concept, & restates definitions according to essential attributes | Student discuss type & number of hypotheses |

In this learners can work individually as well as in groups. It is described that the learner work initially as individuals and later in groups.

### *Unorganized Materials Model*

In this model learners attain concepts from materials that are not organized. The process for attaining concepts in this model involves the following steps: locating the concepts, identifying the attributes used, discussing the adequacy and appropriateness of the attributes and comparing the examples to other passage using the same concept.

Table- Presents the syntax to the model.

The third version of concept attainment is more of a group discussion than an instructional exercise such a Reception and Selection variations. The teacher's role is to facilitate discussion and ensure that it focuses on the development of a concept in the material.

**Table Syntax of Unorganized Materials Model**

| Phase : I | Phase : II |
|---|---|
| Description of Concepts as it is used | Evaluation of concepts |
| Locate and Label conceptIdentify attributes being used. | Discuss adequacy and appropriateness of the concepts being used.Compare examples to other using same concept |

Students discuss the role of hypotheses & attributes

### ***Instructional and Nurturing Effects of the Concept Attainment Model***

The concept Attainment Strategies can accomplish several instructional goals, depending on the emphasis of a particular lesson. They are designed for instruction on specific concepts and on the nature of concepts. They also provide practices in inductive reasoning and opportunities for altering and improving student's concepts building strategies. Finally especially with abstract concepts, the strategies nurture an awareness of alternative perspectives, sensitivity to logical reasoning in communication and a tolerance of ambiguity.

### **Applicability of the Concept Attainment Model :-**

The concept attainment model can be used with students of all ages. Since concrete concepts are taught in early grades, the model is quite appropriate in helping children to learn these concrete concepts. However, the third phase of the model-analysis of thinking strategy is not very feasible with young children. This phase can be used with students from upper primary classes onwards. Further the Reception Model is very appropriate for young children whereas the Selection and Unorganized strategies are more useful in secondary grades. The model is also an excellent tool for evaluation. The phase two of the model tests the attainment of the concepts by asking for additional examples and labeling the given examples.

There is lot of empirical evidence available in the research studies showing the effectiveness of the Concept Attainment Model in teaching Mathematics, Biology and other science subjects and the teachers can make use of this model to help the students for better conceptualization of the subject matter.

### **Examples of concept attainment model**

Teacher ***teaches*** topic 'Quadrilateral' by concept attainment model by following element as per suggested by Bruner

***First Element -Name of concept :- Quadrilateral***

***Second Element- Examples :- ( Positive & Negative)***

Teacher draws some positive & negative diagram on black-board.

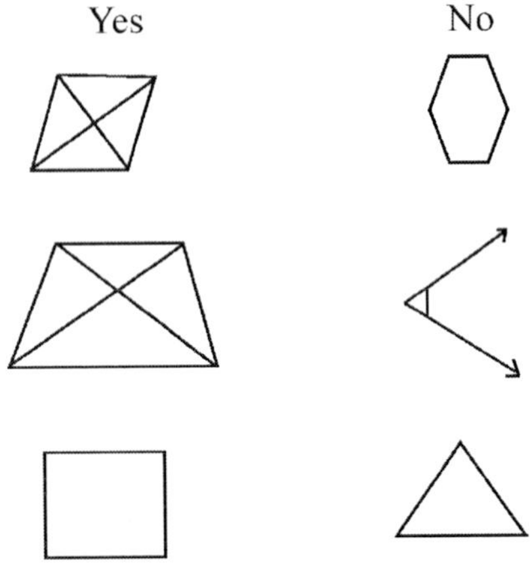


Students observes all diagram of Yes and No types drawn on black board at the same time they takes all common properties / characterstics found in to consideration and compares them with negative diagram.

**Third Element- Attributes -** ( Essential and Non essential)

Teacher asks common properties found by students in yes typed diagram.

**Student -** Essential Attributes

1. Closed diagram
2. four sides, four angles and four vertex
3. one planed diagram
4. Two diagonals

**Fourth Element:- Non Essential Attributes :**

1. measures of each angles
2. measures of each sides
3. Variation in shape of diagram

Teacher asks to students, try to say attributes value of quadrilateral

**Student -** There is a variation in shape of yes typed diagram.

Teacher tells attributes value of quadrilateral are -square, rectangle, parallelogram etc but also clears that there are some concepts in mathematics whose attributes do not have a range of values

**Fifth element**

Rule -

Teacher asks students to tie all common features of yes typed diagram in one difination or rule.

Student tries at their best level

**Student :-** Quadrilateral is closed figure with four sides, angles and vertex.

In this way teacher can teach the concepts likes triangle, parallel lines, circle, angles and its types also.

In the teaching of algebric concept, polynomial, types of sets like empty set, finite and infinite set, equal set, Quadratic Equations, prime and compound numbers can be taught by concept attainment model.

**Example No.-2**

Teaching of Topic 'Prime Numbers' by concept attainment model as follow

**First element-Name of Concept -** Prime Numbers

**<u>Second element :-</u>**

examples ( Positive & Negative)

Teacher writes first set of positive and negative examples on black board

YES

| No. | Number | ' Divisor |
|---|---|---|
| 1 | 5 | 1,5 |
| 2 | 3 | 1,3 |
| 3 | 11 | 1,11 |
| 4 | 23 | 1,23 |
| 5 | 83 | 1,83 |

No

| No. | Number | Divisor |
|---|---|---|
| 1 | 4 | 1,2,4 |
| 2 | 12 | 1, 2,3,4,6 |
| 3 | 21 | 1,3,7,21 |
| 4 | 15 | 1,3,5 |
| 5 | 28 | 4,7,14,28 |

***Teacher***

Observe examples of all yes typed and compare them with 'No' typed examples. Prepare hypothesis and write it into your notebook.

Student prepare hypothesis and verify it.

Teacher again writes another set of examples.

***Teacher***

Verify your hypothesis with the second set of 'Yes' and 'No' typed examples. and list the essential and non essential attributes.

Student says essential attributes.

Teacher list the essential attributes essential attributes told by the student.

***Third Element:- Essential attributes***

Number 1 and itself number are only devisor. **Fourth Element** :-Non Essential attributes -Number 1 and with that another numbers are also devisor.

***Teacher***

with essential attributes we can say that numbers are Prime numbers.

**Rule/Definition**

***Teacher***

Prepare defination for Prime number. **Student :-**

Numbers who have devisior as 1 and that number self are called as prime numbers.

## 2.2.3 Advance Organizer Model

Ausubel is one of the few educational psychological address himself simultaneously to learning, teaching and curriculum. His theory of Meaningful Verbal Learning deals with three concerns: (1) how knowledge (curriculum content) is organized (2) how the mind works top process new information (learning) and (3) how teachers can apply these ideas about curriculum and learning when they present new material to students (instruction). Advance Organizer Model was developed based on Ausubel's Theory of Meaningful Verbal Learning. The structure of this model closely resembles the lecture method. The Advance Organizer Model can be used only for verbal teaching. It can also be used for developing instructional material.

***Theoretical Basic and Assumption***

David P. Ausubel propounded the Theory of Meaningful Verbal Learning. This theory applies to situation where teacher plays the role of lecturer. Its major purpose is to help students acquire subject matter. The teacher is responsible for presenting what is to be learned. Ausubel disagrees with the assumption that meaningful material cannot be presented but must come through independent problem-solving and manipulative experience. According to Ausubel, whether material is meaningful learning takes place if the learner begins with the right set and if the material is potentially understandable. Therefore, meaningful learning involves two things: first, the learner's disposition to relate the new material non-arbitrarily and substantively to his cognitive structure; second, the material he learns should be related to his structure of knowledge on a non-arbitrarily and non-verbatim basis. The key to meaning involves solidly connecting the new learning material with existing ideas in the learner's cognitive structure. In other word, we must relate and reconcile what we known with what we are learning. Meaningful learning thus obviously depends on two principle factors that are both on the material to be learned and on the nature of the particular learner's cognitive structure. According to Ausubel, cognitive structure means a person's knowledge of a particular subject matter at any given time and how well organized, clear and stable it is. In other words, cognitive structure has to do with what kind of knowledge of fields is in our minds, how much of it there is and how well organized it is.

Ausubel (1963) believes that there is parallel between the way the subject matter is organized and the way people organize knowledge in their minds (cognitive structure). He emphasizes that each of the academic discipline has a structure of concepts that are organized hierarchically. Ausubel (1963) conceptualizes a discipline as a level of hierarchically organized concepts that begin with perceptual data at the bottom and proceed through increasing levels of abstractness to the most abstract concept at the top. Thus we may imagine a discipline as begin composed of a pyramid of concept all linked together, with the most concrete concepts at the bottom and more abstract concept the top.

Ausubel (1963) describe the mind as an information-processing and information storing system that can be compared to the conceptual structure of academic disciplines. The mind is a hierarchically organized set of ideas that provides anchors for new information and ideas as that are received, and serve as store house for them. As this information processing system acquires new information and new ideas it recognizes itself to accommodate those ideas. Thus the system is in a continuous state of change. Ausbel maintains that new ideas can be usefully learned and retained only to the extent that they can be related to already available concepts or propositions that provide ideational anchors. If the new material conflicts too strongly with the exiting cognitive structure or is so unrelated that no linkage is provide, the information or ideas may not be incorporated or retained. To prevent this from occurring, the teacher must organize a sequence of knowledge and present it in such a way that the ideational anchors are provide. In additional, the learner must activity reflect on the new material thinking through these linkages, recording differences and discrepancies and discrepancies with existing information and nothing similarities.

Ausubel's ideas about subject matter and cognitive structure have important and direct implications for the organization of curriculum and for instructional procedures. Two principles are suggested for programming content in the subject fields in such a way that the concepts become a stable part of a student's cognitive structure. The first is progressive differentiation and the seconds is integrative reconciliation. Progressive differentiation means that the most general ideas of the disciplines are presented first followed by a gradual increase in detail and specificity. Integrative reconciliation means that the new ideas should be consciously related to previously learned content. In other words the sequence of the curriculum is organized to that each successive learning is carefully related to what has been presented before. If the entire learning material has been conceptualized and presented according to progressive differentiation, then the integrative reconciliation follows naturally, though not without some intent on the teacher's part gradually, as a result of these principles, the discipline is built into the mind of the learner. It must be kept in mind that the discipline and the sequence of instruction are built from the top down, rather than the from the bottom up, first presenting the most inclusive concepts, principles and/or proposition.

### *Advance Organizer-Definition and Types*

An Advance organizer Model begins with the presentation of an Advance Organizer. According to Ausubel (1978), advance organizer is an introductory material at a higher level of abstraction, generality and inclusiveness that the learning material presented before the actual learning task. The main purpose of this is to explain, integrate and interrelate the material in the learning task with previously learned material as well as to help the learners discriminate the new material fro, previously learned material. An advance organizer statement is designed to introduce the material that follows, and is board enough to encompass this information if actual learning task and it helps in organizing the relationship between previous and new knowledge.

There are two types of advance organizers-expository and comparative. Expository organizers are used when the new learning material is completely unfamiliar. They are especially helpful because they provide identical scaffolding for unfamiliar material. Comparative organizers on the other hand, are used most with relatively familiar material. They are designed to integrate new concepts with basically similar concepts existing in the cognitive structure. Concepts existing in the cognitive structure. They are also designed to discriminate between the old and new concepts in order to prevent confusion caused by their similarity.

### *Characteristics of Advance Organizer Model*

According to Mayer (1979) the Advance Organizer Models have the following characteristics.

- Short set of verbal or visual information
- Presented prior to a larger body of to be learned content
- Contain no content from the to-be-learned information
- Provide a means of generating logical relationship among elements in the to-be-learned information
- Influence the learner's encoding process.

### *Syntax of the Advance Organizer Model*

The Advance Organizer Model has three phases of activity and is presented in table

Phase one is the presentation of the advance organizer. This phase consist of three activities: clarifying the aims of the lesson, presenting the advance organizer and promoting awareness of relevant knowledge. Phase two is the presentation of the learning task or material. In this place an important task is maintain student's attention. Another task is to make the organization of the learning material explicit to the students, so that they have an overall sense of direction. Furthermore, the logical order of the material is to-be-made explicit so that the students can see how the ideas relate to each other.

The purpose of phase three is to anchor the new learning material in the student's existing cognitive structure. Ausubel identifies four activities in this phase

Promoting integrative reconciliation
Promoting active reception learning
Eliciting a principle approach to subject mater
Clarification

**Syntax of the Advance Organizer Model**

| Phase I | Phase II | Phase III |
|---|---|---|
| Presentation of Advance Organiser | Presentation of Learning Task or Material | Strengthening cognitive organization |
| Classify aims of the lesson Present Organizer | Make organization explicit | Use principles of intregrativ reconciliation |
| Identify defining attributes | Make logical order of learning material explicit | Promote active reception learning |
| Give examples Provide context Repeat | Maintain attention Present material | Elicit critical approach to subject matter Clarity |

***Social System***

The model has a high structure. In this model the teacher defines roles and controls social and interactive system. However, the learning structure is ideally much more interactive, with students initiating many question and comments.

***Principles if Reaction***

The teacher is seen as presenter of the learning material. The teacher's reaction will be guided by the purpose of clarifying the meaningful of the new learning material, differentiating it from and reconciling it with existing knowledge, making it personally relevant to the student and helping to promote a critical approach to knowledge. Ideally, student will initiate their own question in response to their own drive for meaning.

***Support System***

The organizer and a hierarchical system of knowledge must be developed. Learning material must be organized to that it pertains to the organizer.

### *Applicability of the Model*

The advance Organizer Model was designed for use in face-to face teaching in the form of lectures and explanation. This model can be used in developing instructional material. This model has great potential in teaching concepts, relationship and imparting information effectively. It can be used to teach any subject. Perhaps this model may be very effectively for high school and higher secondary school students.

## 2.2.4 5E Learning Mode

The 5E's is on instructional model based on the constructivist approach to learning, which says that learners build or construct new ideas on top of their old ideas. The 5E's can be used with student of all ages, including adults.

Each of the 5E's describes a phase of learning and each phase begins with the letter 'E' Engage, Explore, Explain, Elaborates and Evaluate the SES allows students and teacher to experience common activities, to use and build on prior knowledge and experience to construct meaning and to continually asses their understanding of a concept.

### *Engage*

This phase of the 5E starts the process. An Engage activity should do the following.

1. Make connections between past and present learning between experience.
2. Anticipate activities and focus students thinking on learning outcomes of current activities. Students should become mentally engaged in the concepts, process or skill to be learned.

### *Explore*

This phase of 5E's provides students with a common base of experience. They identify and develop concepts, process,and skills. During this phase, students activity explore their environment or manipulate materials.

***Explain***

This phase of the 5E's helps students explain. They have been exploring. They have oppurtunities to verbalize their conceptual understanding or to demon strate new skills or behaviour. This phase also provides opportunities for teachers to introduce formal items, phase also provides opportunities for teacher to introduce formal terms, definitions and explanations for concept, process skills or behaviours

***Elaborate***

This phase of the 5E's extends students conceptual understanding and allows them to practice skills and behaviors. Through new experience the learners develop deeper and broader understandings of major concepts obtain more information about areas of interest & refine their skills.

***Evaluate***

This phase of the 5E's encourages learners to assess their understanding and abilities and lets teacher evaluate students understanding of key concepts and skills development.

## 2.3 PLANNING ORGANISING AND MAINTAINING MATHEMATICS LABORATORY

### Mathematics Laboratory

It is true that the mathematics laboratory has not yet received the same general acceptance as a science laboratory. This is probably because the mathematics teachers themselves have not organized the significance of mathematics laboratory as the science teachers have "Actually most of mathematical teacher have been very passive as to this respect.

### 2.3.1 Need of Planning and Organising Mathematics Laboratory

However, recently laboratory work in mathematics is receiving increasing attention. The underlying idea of mathematical laboratory is that pupil will develop. New concept and understanding particularly well through experimental activities dealing with concrete situations. Mathematics concept can be learned better through observation of concepts situations and experiments and manipulation of concrete objects.

Activities such as measuring and drawing, counting weighing and estimating taking the reading from instruments, recording, comparing, analyzing, classifying and checking data, collecting data, working with data and so on will be involved in planning and organizing of mathematical laboratory work.

However, unless proper precautions laboratory work in mathematics may degenerate in to more or less aimless playing with instruments, models and gadgets to be productive, the activist must be carefully planned, supervised and guided towards definite goals. Responsibility for the success and effectiveness of the laboratory work solely rests upon the mathematics teacher activities involved in the laboratory should be classified into two section that are i) demonstration ii) Experimental activities.

In 'Demonstration' some physical instrument or device is used to illustrate and clarify the explanation of a mathematical concept.

Experimental activities include the club of activities which are carried on including or by small group working together.

## 2.3.2 Organisation of Mathematical Laboratory

### *Concrete Method*

The mathematics laboratory should contain material such as beds, pebbles, sticks, ball, frames seeds, balance, weight, measuring tapes, scissors, pins, cardboard, board pins, chart papers, graphpaers, etc.

These material will be very helpful for demonstrating elementary mathematical concepts.

### *Picture & charts*

Picture and Charts plays a Important role in mathematics laboratory. Picture of mathematicians chart shows their contributions,

History and biographic of mathematicians are also very useful in inspiring students and can be placed in the mathematics laboratory.

### *Model*

Various mathematical models which will offer opportunities for student to explore and investigate should be placed in the mathematical laboratory.

### *Bulletin Board*

There should be at least one bulletin board in the mathematics laboratory to display various illustration concerning mathematics information relating to mathematics and its application collected from different sources like magazines, journals and newspapers can be displayed for the benefit of all pupils.

### *Instrument and Equipments*

In mathematics laboratory drawing instruments are necessary to draw and sketch geometrical figures graphs and so on. Therefore in every mathematics laboratory there should be a set of drawing instrumentals like compass, rulers, protractor etc.

### *Weighing and Measuring Instrument*

Mathematical laboratory work quite often involves the important activities of weighing and measuring. Therefore, instrument for measuring and weighing such as measuring tapes, balances of different types, measuring jars and graduated cylinder should be there in a mathematical laboratory.

### *Surveying Instruments*

Surveying is an important aspect of mathematical laboratory. Laying out right angles finding the angular distances, estimating the height of building, finding the angle of elevation and depression are all useful activities which make use of surveying instruments. The following instruments are very useful in this regard and they should have a place in the mathematics laboratory.

- Angle mirror for laying out right angles in the field.
- Sextant for measuring.
  - (*i*) The angular distance.
  - (*ii*) Angles of elevation & depression.
  - (*iii*) The height of on object.
  - (*iv*) The width of river etc.

***Computing Devices***

Student needs to do the computation with speed and accuracy. In order to achieve this mathematics laboratory should have calculating devices like slide rules and calculations.

***Computers***

In this technological age one cannot overestimate the role of computers in the mathematical work. A computer is an effective device for storing information; analyzing and interpreting data. Therefore it is desirable to have computer in the mathematics laboratory to facilitate easy functioning of the mathematical laboratory.

### 2.3.3 Maintaining Mathematical Laboratory

To create interest in mathematics in student there should be mathematics laboratory in each school and Junior College. Mathematics is an essentially subject; where doing is more important than reading. That is why a certain amount of equipment is indispensible in order to make even a start in this subject. More ever; it is felt by a vast majority of people that mathematics is dry and difficult subject; full of abstract thing. The result is that student take very little interest in it. To create the necessary interest is a constant problem for the teacher. This subject demands the use of credits at every step.

Personal equipment should be in large numbers in laboratory. Personal equipments includes instruments which the students can frequently use for his individual work. for example - geometrical box.

Mathematical equipment should be made available through mathematics laboratory as far as possible. expense on such equipment and supplies for athletics, sciences, fine and Industrial arts and crafts. School authorities and administrators should give up the wrong attitude that mathematics is not listed among the laboratory subjects.

Some place for storage is a prerequisite of mathematics laboratory. There must be some almirahs and a room to store and stock the articles before any purchase of the things is made. The place may be provided by having an almirahs in every classroom or by having a few almirahs in one room.Without having proper place and handling the material looses half its age. The things will remain scattered, unarranged, exposed to dust etc.

Issuing of equipment should be proper as per structure of laboratory. If there is central laboratory then issuing should be under supervision of mathematics teacher.

Some clever an active student be appointed for issuing. There should be special time for issuing i.e. before starting school and returning of equipment should be before leaving school. Special notices regarding handling the equipment should be permanently displayed in laboratory.

In this way mathematics laboratory can be maintain.

## 2.4 LEARNING RESOURCES OF MATHEMATICS

Nowadays world has become global village. Information regarding any issue; we get within seconds through Internet. There are so many resources of knowledge via Internet like Websites, Wikipedia e-library but till we have to take another basic resource like Text book, Library, Workbooks as learning resources

When we think about learning resources of mathematics; we can classify them as follows

- Print resources
- E-resources- online & offline

### Print resources are as follows

1. Mathematics library.
2. Text book.
3. Workbook.

## 2.4.1 Mathematics Library

Mathematics library is one of the important sources of acquiring mathematical knowledge and skill. It severs the purpose inculcating good reading and study habits which help in promoting self study and independent work among students.

The students at a young age should be exposed to the joy of reading and should be equipped with the advent of information technology andcyber cafes. there is a growing define in the reading of books. The different types of books available in the mathematics library help the students in promoting reading habits.

### *Need and Functions of a Good Mathematics Library*

Even though there is a general library with a separate section for mathematics Department in every institution, it is necessary to have a separate library for mathematics for the following reasons.

- To provide immediate access to the necessary mathematics books.
- To facilitate timely use and inculcate reference skills.
- To help the mathematics teacher to get acquainted with the latest development in mathematics and innovative techniques of teaching.
- To promote efficiency in the organization of library services.
- To provide a sense of separate identity to mathematics.
- To motivate the students to team mathematics with genuine interest.

### *A Mathematics Library Serves the following Education Purpose*

- A mathematics library provides the extra information necessary for mathematics since a teacher of mathematics may not find time to go beyond the prescribed textbooks.
- Mathematics learning requires a lot of drill, a particular set of textbooks cannot serve this purpose.

- The different types of problems and approaches type of problems and approaches available in different books help the students in developing their problem solving ability and adopting different approaches to problem solving thus making them more open minded and independent.
- Class room teaching may leave many gaps and doubts unclarified. A good library provides opportunities for filling up the gaps and removing the doubts.
- It provides facilities for the gifted students to satisfy their curiosity and thirst for knowledge.

## 2.4.2 The Mathematics Text book

The mathematics text book is another important source of learning mathematics and it plays a key role in effective teachings and learning. Therefore it is important that these text-books do not merely supply information and facts, but also enable the students to understand and appreciate concepts and principles and their relevance in our day to day life.

A text book should stimulate reflective thinking and develop problem solving ability among students. The textbook should present real learning situations which are challenging and interesting for the students and should not render itself as a means of rote learning.

***Need of Text book as a resource Rule of Textbook of Mathematics as a resource***

Though there are contradicting openings regarding use of text book for mathematics teaching and learning the following points support the rule of mathematics text book as a resource.

- A text book provide insight to the teacher in planning the lesson, in selecting the problems to be worked out, the method of teaching to be adopted and the teaching aids to be used.
- The logical and psychological sequence followed in text book helps the teacher in presenting the subject matter in an orderly and systematic sequence.

- A mathematics text book provide the teacher with the basic information considered essential in attaining the objectives of mathematics educational and this helps the teacher to plan appropriate learning experiences. Text book provides important source of materials for reviewing and recapitulating the lesions taught in the class.
- Textbook provide adequate material for drill and practice and thus helps in fixing the mathematical principles and formulae in the minds of the students.
- The textbook helps in the extensive study of the subject as it presents different problems & various approaches to problem solving.

### 2.4.3 Workbook

A workbook is the modification of the text book and is slowly coming in to the mathematics classroom. A workbook should be written by an experienced teacher with care and foresight.

**Functions of Workbook**

- It suggests appropriate activities and exercise in addition to what the text book does.
- It saves time for the students of they need not recopy the problems and exercise form the text book. It eliminates the mistakes due to the wrong copying of numbers and digits.
- It facilitates uniformity in student's work and facilities easy correction of their work.
- It serves as a supplementary teaching device.
- It provides activities and exercise in addition to the text book problems and exercise.
- Slow learners can learn at their own place.

***Characteristics of Workbook***

- It should be written by an experienced teacher of mathematics.

- The author should clearly specify the educational outcome that he tries to bring about.
- A variety of well graded experience should be provided for each topic.
- Enough space should be provided in the book far working out the problems.
- The exercise should cater to the individual differences and individual needs.
- It should be accompanied by a list of answers to various graded assignment or experience given in the work book to enable the pupils to verify their answers.
- It can be made attractive and appealing by suitable illustrations and diagram.

### 2.4.5 Mathematics Club

Mathematics club plays an important role in motivate the students to learn mathematics with interest and involvement. Sometimes mathematics teaching in classroom becomes so monotonous that the student become restless and get easily distracted. Mathematics club provides excellent opportunities for students to break away from the monotomy of a rigid and structured classroom environment. Though the leaning that takes place in a mathematics club is informal in nature. In mathematics club the student choose activity on his own and persue them in a free and relaxed manner contrary to the atmosphere prevailing in a classroom. Club provides a lot of freedom of expression for the students & it supplement classroom learning.

***Functions of the Mathematics Club***

- It Mathematics club helps in the proper utilities of leisure time.
- It helps in arousing and maintaining student's interest to mathematics.
- It provides the students with opportunities to develop their explorative, creative and inventive faculties.

- It inculcates the habit of self study and independent work among the student.
- It offers an ideal avenue for free exchange of mathematical ideas and for frank and helpful criticism of these ideas.
- It provides an informal and social atmosphere which the classroom can hardly provide.
- It helps in developing heuristic and problem solving attitude among the students.
- It provides opportunities for students to translate the theory into practice and to apply their learning in daily life situations.
- It offers a good platform for student to listen to renowned mathematics, eminent mathematics teachers and educationists and to acquaint themselves and educationist and to acquaint themselves with the latest developments in mathematics.
- Mathematics club extend learning beyond the limits of classroom. Though clubs may meet during school to out of school hours at home, in the laboratory in the field etc.

### *Organization of Mathematics Club*

Usually the initiative for the organization of mathematics club should come the students but in absence of it a mathematics teacher should take the lead first of all this matter he would take into confidence the head of Institution seek his approval. Then he should approach the fellow teachers for their co-operative start discussing the need of establishing a mathematics club with individual students. After creating a suitable environment he should call a meeting of all interested students. They should be told about the advantages of mathematics club with all such foundations, teacher should now actually move for its formal organizations and working.

### *Formal Organization*

Members of Mathematics club should be as follow.

1. Principle or Headmaster as its patron.
2. A senior but interested teacher of mathematics of Adviser.

3. All the mathematics student of the school can be members of the club. Those student who are interested in mathematics can be the associate members who wants to play key rule in running of club activity can take the responsibility like.
   (*a*) President.
   (*b*) Vice President.
   (*c*) Secretary.
   (*d*) Treasurer.

The advisor should property acquaint all, the students with their functions and responsibilities.

**Working of Mathematics Club**

The program of mathematics clubs may cover a wide range of topics. The topics way include history of mathematics, biographical sketches evolution and development of certain aspects of Presents days mathematics, some selected topics from any branch of mathematics games and contrast and application of mathematics to other subjects and fields of activity. The Nature of the programs and topics will depend upon the age and advancement of the members of the club the sources & facilities available and the advantage drawn from such programs. It is desirable to plan the program for the whole session.

Some of the activities that can be undertaken by mathematics club may be of following types.

- Mathematical exhibitions & fairs.
- Lectures on important topics of mathematics by eminent scholars and teachers.
- Celebration of historical days and events of mathematical significant.
- Inter school contest & quiz competitions on topics of mathematics interest.
- Establishment and Maintenance of mathematical laboratory.
- Preparation of charts, models and improvised apparatus for the mathematics laboratory.

- Programmers for listening to the radio broadcast on topics of mathematics interest.
- Telecast of ugc programs on mathematics.
- Field work & field trips to the places of mathematical interest.
- Article writing related to mathematics for the school magazine or newsletters.
- Recreational activities in mathematics such a puzzles riddles, catch problems.
- Publication of newsletter & bulletin of the club.

### 2.4.6 Introduction to Mathematics Software – Mathcad and Geogebra

***MathCad***

Mathcad is a computer Software primarily intended for the verification, validation, documentation and re-use of engineering calculations. First introduced in 1986 on DOS. It was the first to introduce live editing of typeset mathematical notation, combined with it automatic computations.

Mathcad, Parametric Technology Corporation's engineering calculation solution, is used by engineers and scientists in various disciplines- most often those of mechanical, chemical, electrical, and civil engineering. Originally conceived and written by Allen Razdow. Mathcad is new owned by PTC and is generally accepted as the first computer application to automatically compute and check consistency of engineering units such as the international system of Units (SI) throughout the entire set of calculations. Mathcad today includes some of the capabilities of a computer algebra system, but remains oriented towards ease of use and simultaneous documentation of numerical engineering applications.

Mathcad is oriented around a worksheet in which equations and expressions are created and manipulated in the same graphical format in which they are presented as opposed to authoring in plain text, an approach later adopted by other systems such as Mathematica and Maple. Mathcad is part of a broader product developed system often utilized for the many analytical touch point within the systems engineering process.

### *Applications of Mathcad*

The Mathcad interface allows to combine a variety of different elements (Mathematics, descriptive text, and supporting imagery) into the form of a worksheet, which is naturally readable. Because the mathematics are core to the program, the math is inherently live, dynamically recalculating as upstream values are alerted. This allows for simple manipulation of input variables, assumptions, and expressions, which in turn update in real time. The examples below serve to outline the scope of Mathcad's capabilities, rather than to give specific details on the individual product functionality.

- Utilize numerous numeric functions, across examples such as statistics, data analysis, image processing and signal processing.
- Automatically manage Units throughout the worksheet, preventing improper operations and performing automatic unit-reduction
- Finds roots of polynomials and functions
- Calculate and manipulate expressions symbolically, including within system of equations
- Create parametric 2D and 3D Plot types, as well as discrete date plots
- Perform curve fitting and regression analysis on experimental dataset

Although Mathcad is mostly oriented to non programming users, it is also used in more complex projects to visualize results of mathematical modeling by using distributed computing and coupling with programs written using more traditional languages such as C++.

### *Geogebra*

Is an interactive geometry, algebra, statistics and calculus application, intended for learning and teaching mathematics and science from primary school to university level. Geogebra is available on multiple platform with its desktop application for Windows, Mac OS and Linux with, its tablet apps for Android, iPad and Windows, and with its web application based on HTML5 technology.

Its creator, Markus Hohenwarter, started the project in 2001 at the university of Salzburg, continuing it at Florida Atlantic University (2006-2008) Florida State University (2008-2009), and now at the University of Lizn together with the help of open-source developers and translators all over the world.

After a successful Kickstarter campaign, Geogebra expanded their offerings to include an iPad an Android and a Windows Store appversion.

In 2013, Bernard parisse's Giac was integrated into GeoGebra's CAS view.

GeoGebra continues to expand its efforts to deliver the best possible dynamic mathematics software and services to students and teachers worldwide, with a community of users that extend to all but a few countries. Geogebra includes both a commercial and not-for-profit entity, working closely together from head office in Linz, Austria to continue to expand the software and cloud services available to its user community of student, teacher and growing network of government partners.

***Interactive geometry, algebra, statistics and calculus -***

GeoGebra is interactive mathematics software for learning and teaching mathematics and science form primary school up to university level. Constructions can be made with points, vectors, segments, lines, polygons, conic sections, inequalities, implicit polynomials and functions. All of them can be changed dynamically afterwards. Elements can be entered and modified directly via mouse and touch, or through the Input Bar. Geogebra has the ability to use variables for numbers, vectors and points, find derivatives and integrals of function and has a full complement of and to understands like Root of Extremum. Teacher and students can use Geogebra to make conjectures and to understand how to prove geometric theorems.

**Its main features are**

- Interactive geometry environment (2D and 3D)
- Built-in spreadsheet
- Built-in CAS
- Built-in statistics and calculus tools
- Allows scripting
- Large number of interactive learning and teaching resources at Geogebra Materials

### *GeoGebra Materials Platform*

Dynamic Geogebra applets can be directly uploaded to the Geogebra related Materials platform, the official cloud services and repository of Geogebra related and interactive learning and teaching resources. GeoGebra Materials was initially launched under the names GeoGebra Tube in June 2011 and renamed in 2016. With recent improvement and extend functionality the services now hosts more than 1 million resources (April 2016), 400,000+ of which are shared are shared publicity as searchable materials - such as interactive worksheets, simulations, games and e-books created using the GeoGebra Book feature.

Geogebra materials can be also exported in several formats, including as static images or as Animated GIF. SVG vector images can be further edited using third party software, e.g. Inkscape. EMF vectors formats can be directly imported in several Office application. There are also option for exporting to the system clipboard, PNG, PDF, EPS. GeoGebra can also crearrrted code that can be used inside LaTex files through its PSTricks, PGF/TikZ and Asymptote export options.

### *Math lab*

Math Lab is a novel concept which enables students to learn and explore mathematical concepts and verify mathematical facts and theorems through a variety of activities using different materials. These activities may be carried out by the teacher or the student to explore, to learn, to stimulate interest and develop favorable attitude towards mathematics. Math Lab is specially crafted in accordance to the NCERT guidelines that focus on learning by doing. It inculcates learning through 'Applied Reasoning'. It inspires out of the box thinking and provides an opportunity to explore the valuable knowledge with classmate. New education policy of mathematics recommended that 20 percent of the marks to be allocated to each student from the lab Assessments, towards the final marks.

Based on the three pillars of 'Imagination, Investigation and Interaction', It provides an opportunity to student to understand, Internationalize, discover and verify the basic mathematical and geometrical concepts through concrete objects and situations, thus building interest and confidence in students learning the subjects. The concept of mathlab intended as a mathematics learning enhancement program for elementary schools.

***Need and Purpose of Math lab***

Some of the ways in which a Math Lab can contribute to the learning of the subjects are :

- It provides an opportunity to students to understand and internationalize the basic mathematical concepts through concrete objects and situations.
- It enables the students to verify or discover several geometrical properties and facts using models or by paper cutting and folding techniques.
- It helps the students to build interest and confidence in learning the subjects'
- The laboratory provides opportunity to exhibit the relatedness of mathematical concepts with everyday life.
- It provides scope for individual participation in the process of learning and becoming autonomous learner.
- It provides scope for greater involvement of both the mind and the hand which facilitate cognition.

- The Math Lab allows and encourages the students to think, discuss with each other and the teacher and assimilate the concepts in a more effective manner.
- It enables the teacher to demonstrate, explain and reinforce abstract mathematical ideas by using concrete objects, models, charts, graphs, pictures, posters, etc.

***Physical Infrastructure, materials and human resources***

It is necessary that every school have a mathematic laboratory with a general design and layout. The minimum material required to be kept in the laboratory may include furniture, all essential equipment, raw materials and other necessary things to carry out the activities. It is desirable that a person with minimum qualification of graduation (with mathematics as one of the subjects) and professional of the mathematics laboratory. He/she is expected to have special skills and interest to carry out practical work in the subject. The concerned mathematics teacher will accompany the class to the laboratory and the two will jointly conduct the desired activities. A laboratory attendant or laboratory assistant with suitable qualification and desired knowledge in the subject can be added an advantage.

***Time allocation for activities***

It is desirable that about 15%-20% of the total available time for mathematics be devoted to activities. Proper allocation of periods for laboratory activities may be made in the time table. The total available time may be divided judiciously between theory classes and practical work.

***Scheme of Evaluation***

20% weightage will be given to the internal assessment in the subject. The following pattern is given by Board's theory examination and school based internal assessment for all standards means from 5 to 12

Theory examination: 80 Marks

Internal assessment: 20 Marks

Internal assessment of 20 Marks, based on school -based examination, will have the following break -up

Year-end assessment of activities: 10 marks

Assessment of project work: 5 marks

Continuous assessment: 5 marks

Assessment of Activity Work

## 2.5 COMPETENCIES OF MATHEMATICS TEACHER

Everything in education is planned and set for the benefit of the students. They are to bee given varied learning experience for the modification of their behavior and development of their personalities. Different subject of the curriculum contribute towards the realization of this aim. Like other subject in teaching of mathematics many things are planned and set in advance. Curriculum and syllabus are farmed, new techniques and devices are explored variety of audio and visual aids are collected, appropriate text books are written various equipments are purchased and suitable facilities for the effectives learning are provided. In spite of all these preparations and planning the most important thing that can never be challenged and matched for the presence of a competent and effective teacher. No machine and no other source how sophisticated it may be replace him. He will always hold the key position.

Thereby quality of mathematics education to a great extent will definitely be determined by the competencies of mathematics teacher. How the question arises what type of mathematics teachers should be there to our schools for the effective realization of the aims and objectives of a mathematics teacher and what should be the competencies of mathematics teacher and what may be expected from him for being a good mathematics teacher? Let us explore these things.

## Competencies of Mathematics Teacher

**1. Pre-requsite Qualification**

Mastery of the subject is an absolute necessity. The teacher much possesses a fairly high basic qualification in his subject. The level of his knowledge must be much higher than that of the knowledge he is expected to import. Besides a good degree, he should possess a strong aptitude for the subject.

**2. Professional Training**

Before going in, for this training he should make sure that he has an enthusiastic interest in the profession.

During training he should acquaint himself with child psychology, methods of teaching techniques.

As a part of his preparatory training he should observe frequently the classroom work of experienced teacher in the practicing school.

**3. Professional activities**

Mathematics teacher should have habit of reading mathematics. Journals and latest book for professional interest The Teacher may do professional research and write professional articles or books.

The Teacher may take an active part in the programs and discussion of professional organization, committees, study groups and seminars reading mathematics curriculum. He should never think that he has learnt enough for all times.

**4. School Activities**

The effective planning and execution of school activities require the cooperation of individual teachers. The teacher should enthusiastically participate in the following activities.

(*i*) Faculty Meeting.

(*ii*) School Club.

(*iii*) School Publications.

(*iv*) Student Projects.

(*v*) Exhibitions.

(*vi*) Many sided co-operation between department and other department.

**5. Mathematical Organisations**

Mathematics teacher should organize themselves at district, zonal and state levels for mutual professional benefits such on organizations will provide a channel for exchange of ideas & experiences.

**6. Department Duties**

For smooth and efficient functioning of his department each teacher must accept his share of responsibility.

A few common departmental duties are.

(*i*) Participation in departmental meeting and discussion.

(*ii*) Selection and improvement of text books.

(*iii*) Organization and revision of subject curriculum.

(*iv*) Sponsoring of mathematics club.

(*v*) S election and ordering of library books and Periodicals.

(*vi*) Improvement of question papers.

(*vii*) Organization of exhibition contests and assembly Programs.

(*viii*) Taking part in guidance services and remedial classes.

**7. Administrative Duties**

Mathematics teacher has to keep record of attendance, conduct and Performance of Pupils. These records serve administrative, as well as teaching purposes. The result of the student Performance has to be periodically reported to the parents and the administrative officers. Similarly the deficiencies of individual students have to be reported. He uses the result of various test of for diagnostic adjustment and remedial purpose. He has to undertake guidance and counseling work.

**8. Community activities**

Mathematics teacher have maintain relations not only with students but their parents also to improves school community relations. He should take ininative in arranging meeting of social or civic group's parents association and old student's association teacher may also organize and direct local fairs, celebration or festivals they may also organize lectures tournaments naivety program and other activity which are of interest to the community.

**9. Effective teaching**

There is large number of duties related to teaching.

(*i*) Familiarity with the aims and objectives of teachings mathematics at all levels.

(*ii*) Knowledge and use of proper devices and techniques according to the resources and demands of the situations.

(*iii*) Possession of the skills like computation drawing and sketching.

(*iv*) Ability to inculcate interest among the student.

(*v*) Ability to prepare good test to frame me good Problems.

**10. In Service Training**

Mathematics teacher have to take participation in In-service training to improve his teaching skills according new technology and knowledge for this purpose he have always to keep himself with in-service training centers. Like extension service departments, state school education board, NCERT, he should attend not only various meeting and courses with an open mind to learn but also engage in action research regarding their subjects and its teaching.

## Correlation of Mathematics

Nature is the primary source of human knowledge. The various branches of knowledge has been developed as a result of different forms of increasing needs of human being obliviously. There should be some form of correlation among these branches of knowledge. The major aim of education is the all-round and harmonious development of the child. This aims can be achieved through a comprehensive education. The comprehensive education may be the unification of knowledge existing in various branches of learning. To achieve such unification a conscious effort has to be made by the teachers teaching various subjects. A teacher can do so by correlating the knowledge of a subject with other subject and its application in other branches of knowledge or different situations of life.

Mathematics is not only related to all the subjects but it contributes to great extent in the achievement and progress of most of the subject. That is why it is called the science of all the

Sciences. Every branch of knowledge consists of various theories and laws the reliability and validity of these theories depend upon their possibility of presentation in a mathematical form. The numerical form of a fact is always reliable and valid. Thus every branch of knowledge seeks the helps of rules and techniques of mathematics in its progress and development.

## 2.6. NEEDS AND IMPORTANCE OF CORRELATION

The student understand and grasp the content of any subject very easily if it is corrected with the content of other subject for effective learning, the teacher has to take full advantage of various correlation with most of the school subject and other human experience. So it is essential for mathematics teacher to have good knowledge of correlation of mathematics with other subject to make teaching and learning process effective and interesting.

Hence teaching of mathematics should be done keeping in view its correlation with other subjects.

The importance of knowledge of correlation in the teaching of mathematics may be expressed in the following points.

(*i*) The correlation of mathematics helps in developing and maintaining the interest of learners in mathematics.

(*ii*) The correlation of mathematics with other subject works as stimulus to the learners of mathematics.

(*iii*) It provides opportunities for applying the operations of mathematics in the study of other subject.

(*iv*) It helps in removing the isolation of traditional teaching of mathematics.

(*v*) It helps in presenting the various subject in an integrated from at different level of education.

(*vi*) It motivates the students for learning of mathematics.

(*vii*) It provide opportunity to establish perfect coordination between head, heart and hand or between knowing feeling and doing aspects of learning.

(*viii*) The project method, term teaching and problem solving method can be made practical and effective by correlating. The mathematics with other subject.

## Types of correlation

(*i*) Correlation of mathematics with daily life.

(*ii*) Correlation between different branches of mathematics.

(*iii*) Correlation of mathematics with other subjects.

***Correlation of Mathematics with daily life***

It is true that in each every sphere of daily life mathematics provides us its help and patronage without which we cannot do anything. The knowledge of mathematics is very versatile and required in all the day to day life activities beginning from awakening to sleep in night. Today life activities beginning from awakening to sleep in night. Thus we can say that in our daily life, mathematics is as mixed as oxygen in the air. Every dealing of our life begins and ends with mathematical thinking and reasoning. for example; daily house hold problems, food, clothing, idea of quantity and quality, daily account of income and expenditure, allocation of funds etc. such type to day to day problems cannot be completed without the knowledge of mathematics. Young J.W. A. has remarked that "Whenever we turn in these days of iron, steam and electricity we find that mathematics has been the pioneer were its backbone removed, our material civilization would inevitably collapse." Formula and principles of branches in solving the problems of another branch. LCM, GCM, squares fractions, etc. in algebra are based upon the rules of arithmetic. The four fundamental operations of arithmetic additions, substractions, multiplication and division are widely used in all branches of mathematics.

The modern mathematics, applied mathematics and higher mathematics have a lot of bearing upon the elementary rules and regulations of thematic, algebra and geometry. The problems of higher mathematics cannot be solved without a good knowledge of elementary mathematics. Thus it may be said that there is a very high correlation between different branches of mathematics. Therefore it is desirables on the part of the teacher to make it clear to the student that the knowledge of this correlation shall be helpful in the future of study.

***Correlation of Mathematics with other subject :***

Mathematics is the pivot of science It has been very well said that mathematics is a science of all science and art of all arts, In this respect 'Roger Bacon' has remarked that, "Mathematics is the gateway and key of all science" The correlation of mathematics with different branches of science is as follows.

**a. Mathematics and physics**

Mathematics and physics are very closely related and has a very well established correlation. Each rule and principle in physics takes mathematical form and mathematics gives final shape to the rules, laws and principle of physics.

**Eg**

- The laws of motion, friction, expansion of solids, liquid pressure are depedent on mathematics.
- The measurement unit in physics is employed as frequently as in mathematics.
- The coefficient of linear expansion of deferent metal, cubical expansion of liquids, Charles law of expansion of gases, conversion of sales are based on mathematical knowledge.

**b. Mathematics and Chemistry**

Mathematics and chemistry are also correlated and the chemical combinations and their equations are based on mathematics

**Eg**

- In the estimation of elements of organic compound the use of percentage, ratio and proportion is needed.
- Molecular weight and number of organic compound is based on mathematics.

- Balancing of chemical equations and other calculation work is also based on mathematical knowledge.

### *Mathematics and Biology*

A Biologist must have the sufficient knowledge of mathematics to understand its branches like; bio-physics and bio-chemistry.

**Eg**

- The caloric and natrive values of found articles are based on mathematics.
- The rate of respiration, transpiration, supply of water in connection to all living bodies, is related to mathematics.
- Number of bones, organs etc. it is also mathematical.
- Mathematics can acquire knowledge of heredity growth, nutrition, maturation etc.
- Study of living cells composition of blood, age & category of plants, animals is possible through mathematical knowledge.

### *Mathematics and Geography*

The knowledge of mathematics is also applicable to the study of geography for example shape and size of

earth, area, distance of place, height and distance, temperature longitude, time etc. All are based on mathematical calculation, similarly, to study the rivers, canal, mountains, population, climate, depth, drawing of graph and figures moments of winds, falling of rains etc. in all these mathematics plays a prominent role. Hence all the geological and geographical studies are not possible without the proper application of mathematics.

### *Mathematics and History*

The knowledge of History helps in understanding the historical development of mathematics. History and contribution of great mathematics in the field of mathematics similarly mathematical knowledge is applied in history to know the dates, time, day etc. of various historical events.

### *Mathematics and Languages*

As mathematics is subject of all other subject Hence In teaching of all languages knowledge of mathematics is useful for example types of sentence, types of nouns, verb noble wovels. Birth and Death of author, Poem. Similarly mathematics also helps the language in writing and expressing correctly mathematics develops and attitude of exactness in the student which helps in maintaining the correct use of language.

Language is an essential element of teaching no subject can be taught without the use of language. Thus it is also applicable to mathematics. The principles and method of mathematics are expressed through the medium of languages. The symbols, notations and formula used in mathematics are short method of expressing the statement of language. That is why, it is called mathematical language. So it is language that helps the mathematics and its teaching. Thus mathematics and language have significant relationship.

### *Mathematics and Fine Arts*

The basic elements of an art are rhythm, harmony, proportion, balance and symmetry. The proper expression of these elements from the beauty of a piece of art. The above terms or words belong very much to mathematics. Thus mathematics provides a basis and background for aesthetic appreciation. That is why only mathematical mind can appreciate fully a beautiful piece of art, painting architecture, and music. It is very that something like mathematics exists in music similarly, something music exists in doing the exercise of mathematics. The views of prominent philosopher and mathematics also support the relationship of these two discipliners.

According to liability, 'Music is a hidden exercise in arithmetic of mind unconscious of dealing with numbers'

According to W. F. White. "Mathematics too has its triumphs of the creative imagination; its beautiful theorems, its proof and processes whose perfection of forms has made them classic. He must be a 'practical, man who can see no poetry in mathematics"

"Pythagoras says" where harmony is, there are numbers" According to Berlnard Russell, "Mathematics rightly viewed, possesses not only truth but supreme beauty a beauty cold and austere, like that of sculpture, without appeal to any part of our weaker nature, without the gorgeous trapping of painting or music, yet sublimely pure, and capable of a stern perfection such as only the greatest art can slow.

### *Mathematics and Drawing*

Geometrical drawing is an important branch of drawing. In geometrical drawing various principles of geometry are frequently used. The knowledge of geometry also helps in the study of other branches of drawing such as memory drawing; figure drawing etc. on the other hand a good knowledge and efficiency in drawing helps to draw geometrical figures in the study of mathematics. Thus we find that there is close correlation between drawing and mathematics.

### *Mathematics and Commerce*

The knowledge of mathematics helps to understand various concepts and branches of commerce. The basis of banking and accountancy is mathematics. It is considered that without having good knowledge and practice of mathematics No one can't become a good accountant. In commerce calculation of Interest are based on mathematics principle and formulae. Share, debentures mutual funds. Accounting etc. are also based on mathematical calculation. Thus most of knowledge of commerce requires the application of mathematical knowledge.

### *Mathematics and Economics*

Mathematics laws, language, principles and methods are frequently used in describing interpreting and explaining economic phenomena. According to J.B. says, " Economics is the science which trends of wealth" Great economist of Marshal has well remarked that, "The direct application of mathematical reasoning to the discovery of economic truth has recently rendered great services in the hands of master mathematics" In economics mathematical knowledge is applied in many way such as - collection analysis, calculation, interpretation and presentation of data regarding, population investment, income, expenditure, production, banking, business, demand and supply etc.

Various mathematical method are used to economics forecast regarding.

### *Mathematics and Engineering*

It engineering scientific principles and rules are applied to task. It deals with surveying, leveling, designing, estimating, construction etc. The application of mathematics is indispensable in all these process. Thus mathematics makes the foundation of engineering. That is why, at least intermediate or higher secondary with mathematics and physics is a pre qualification fur entering to an engineering course. In all the branches of engineering such as civil, mechanical, electrical, aeronautical etc. mathematical principle are directly applied. By the application of geometrical principles to design and construction the durability of product can be increased.

Thus it is very clear that mathematics and engineering are highly correlated.

### *Correlation between Mathematics and Agriculture*

Not only Modern but traditional agriculture also based on mathematics. The farmer used a certain quantity of a particular seed for sowing in a certain area to get a good crop. Time and season for sowing the seeds, watering the plants at fixed intervals etc. require mathematical knowledge now a days the use of modern technology in agriculture have made it more dependent on mathematics.

Various aspects of agriculture science requires direct application of mathematics, such as measurement of land and area, assessment of production per unit area, cost of labour, time and work, average of return, rates of seed manure etc. mathematics helps a lot in the advanced study of agriculture. Agricultural statistics have been developed as field of study. It helps in agricultural studies and researches. Thus it can be said that there is a good correlation between mathematics and agriculture.

### *Mathematics and Psychology*

Psychology has now been established as a science. It has become possible by applying scientific method to a great extent in its studies. The experimental psychology utilizes scientific principles at every stage. It has become highly mathematical due to use of higher statistical techniques in drawing the inferences. The calculation of measures of central tendency, measures of dispersion, coefficient of correlation probable errors of measurement and testing the significant of different between means and other statistics are very common in its studies.

Intelligent quotient (I.Q.) is very popular phenomenon in psychology. The mathematical formula for finding the I.Q. is

I.Q = Mental Age/Chronological Age'100

I.Q. = M.A./C.A/100

Psychological deals with study of behavior of living organism cannot be easily isolated and experimented upon. No single individual can be representative of whole species so, psychological experiment are generally performed on large groups taken at random. For Interpretation of result, statistical analysis is the only relative method for understanding the psychological phenomena.

### *Mathematics and Philosophy*

In ancient all the subject were taught as a part of philosophy. Mathematics were also taught as a part of philosophy. Most of ancient scientist and mathematicians were philosophers.

Mathematics occupies a central place between natural philosophy and mental philosophy. In mathematics, the philosopher find orderly and systematic achievement of unambiguous truth.

The great philosopher plato and other thinkers came under the influence of mathematics in search of distinction between fact and fiction. Mathematics helps the philosopher in reaching to truth from falsehood. According to A. N. Whitehead philosophers when they have possessed a through knowledge of mathematics, have been among those who have enriched the science with some o its best ideas.

# BIBLIOGRAPHY


1. Yadav Siyaram (2013) -Teaching of Mathematics (7th edition) Agrawal Publication Agra-2
2. Kulshrestha A.K. ( 2014)- Teaching of Mathematics (1st edition) R. LALL Book Depot Meerut.
3. Kulbirsingh Sidhu (1995)- The Teaching of Mathematics (4th revised edition) Sterling Publisher Private Ltd. New Delhi-110020
4. Dr. Mangal S.K. - Teaching of Mathematics (1st edition) Vinod Publication, Ludhiana 141008
5. Roi B. C.- Method- Teaching of Mathematics -Prakashan Kendra, Lucknow-7
6. Dr. James Anice, Dr. Balsubramanian P.S. - (2013) Teaching of Mathematics (Reprint, 1st Edition) Neelkamal Publication Pvt. Ltd. Hyderabad-500095
7. Dr. K.N.Krishna Kumar, Dr.Bondu Raju & Dr.G. Srilata - (1st edition-201 6) Neelkamal Publication Pvt. Ltd.Sultan Bazar, Hyderabad.


♦ ♦ ♦